AROUND the TURN

Race cars careening around yet another turn seem common-place today, but the sport had to maneuver around some daunting roadblocks just to get to the start-finish line and faces more in the future.

In *Around the Turn*, NASCAR historian Bill Lazarus documents NASCAR's greatest triumphs, and some of its more bizarre moments …

- The first unofficial race, where six hardy drivers dodged snowballs and hypothermia

- The arrival of media savvy drivers like Richard Petty who nevertheless led a short-lived strike

- The growth in prestige from early derision to the surprise visit by President Ronald Reagan along with kings and Hollywood royalty

- The 1979 fistfight that sparked media interest and prompted widespread television coverage

- The roadblocks now facing NASCAR as it seeks a wider audience amid rising costs and growing competition

AROUND the TURN

How stock car racing became one of the most popular sports in the United States

WILLIAM P. LAZARUS

boldventurepress.com

Around the Turn
by William P. Lazarus
is an original work of nonfiction,
published for the first time
in this paperback edition.

First Printing
January 2017

© 2017 William P. Lazarus. All Rights Reserved.

ISBN-13: 978-1541090934
Retail cover price $14.95
Available in eBook edition

Printed and bound in the United States.

Published by Bold Venture Press
www.boldventurepress.com

CONTENTS

ACKNOWLEDGEMENTS

This book could not have been completed without the help of several people, including my agent Mark Sullivan, who proposed the idea; Buz McKim, NASCAR Hall of Fame archivist whose knowledge of motorsports and support for my efforts have been unfailing; and Eddie Roche, retired NASCAR archivist who was always ready to offer advice.

Of course, I can't forget my wife, daughter and mother, all of whom have inspired me to keep writing.

However, the biggest thanks has to go to those who built stock car racing from nothing despite some amazing complications that would have silenced the engines of lesser leaders.

DEDICATION

To all the drivers who, with the barest of safety equipment and the lust for speed, pioneered the path NASCAR has followed since its first race in 1949.

INTRODUCTION

U nlikely as it seems, stock car racing was not always one of the most popular sports in America. At one time, more than 100,000-plus fans did not turn up at modern tracks around the country virtually every weekend from February through November to cheer on their favorite drivers. Then, the sport was riveted to a southern base. At one time, International Speedway Corporation wasn't able to spend $600 million to buy 400 acres of land on Staten Island for a possible New York track — the largest construction project the company has ever considered. The idea would have been unthinkable; the finances, impossible; the location, absurd.

The track has never been built, but, for years, NASCAR held its award banquet in the heart of the Big Apple, adding some redneck charm to the skyscrapers and bustling lifestyle.

At one time, tracks were tiny and dirty. Dust flew everywhere as the drivers wrestled with heavy cars and each other in front of a relatively small number of spectators.

The first race sanctioned by National Association for Stock Car Auto Racing (NASCAR), June 19, 1949, in Charlotte, North Carolina, couldn't be seen by most of 13,000 people who reportedly showed up — some of whom climbed the willow tree by turn 3 to get above the dust and obtain a better view.

One long-time racer recalled that historic event in a published interview. "I can't tell you how dusty it was," said Tim Flock, an early NASCAR star who died in 1998. "Some of the scorers missed eight to ten laps because they couldn't see the cars. The track owner, Carl Allison, was sued by the neighbors because there was so much dust on their houses. We had to run our wipers the whole race."

There had to be more cleaning up before this sport was acceptable to the country. And a lot more twists and turns. Almost every decade, sometimes more often, stock car racing ran into a crisis and, somehow, managed to continue down a dimly lit road. Most tracks have four turns: NASCAR history has a lot more.

In the 1930s, two early sponsors lost money and dropped out. In the 1950s, the new sanctioning body had to decide whether to take its drivers onto asphalt or stay with dirt tracks. Then, there was an attempted driver boycott, loss of the automobile industry's support, lack of media coverage, the death of the sports' greatest hero and more.

One by one, stock car racing faced the challenges and thrived. This book will look at all the key races and events that helped boost stock car racing to its current lofty position in the pantheon of American sports. There are a lot of them. Few major professional sports can point to so many significant milestones.

In other sports, famous athletes served as the lodestones. Their histories are built around their heroes. For example, baseball fans identify Babe Ruth's sale to the New York Yankees in 1919 as the most early significant event in that sport along with Jackie Robinson breaking the color barrier in 1947. Golf was boosted by the arrival of Arnold Palmer and his pants-tugging charisma in the 1950s. He was followed by Jack Nicklaus and then Tiger Woods served as the standard bearer for many years. Jordan Spieth looks to be next in line, Basketball rode on the shoulders of Ervin "Magic" Johnston and Larry Bird, starting in 1979, followed by Michael Jordan, Kobe Bryant and LeBron James; Seth Curry seems ready to assume the mantle. For professional football, the magic of Johnny Unitas and the televised 1958 championship game between the Baltimore Colts and the New York Giants seems to have been the catalyst.

The expansion of the National Hockey League in 1968 made that sport relevant.

Stock car racing isn't that limited. One event didn't establish the sport. Each of the events creating a mosaic of a high speed, pageantry-filled sport that has captured the imagination of fans throughout the country and infiltrated every aspect of American culture will be covered in detail with full explanations of why each is significant.

- 1895: The first American race
- 1938: The first race promoted by Bill France
- 1950: The first race on a super speedway
- 1969: The race in which Bill France faced off against a union that threatened NASCAR control
- 1972: The first race in conjunction with the R.J. Reynolds Tobacco Co.
- 1979: The first televised Daytona 500
- 1984: Richard Petty's 200th win with the president of the United States in attendance.
- 1992: Petty's retirement and arrival of Jeff Gordon
- 2001: The death of Dale Earnhardt
- 2001: Kevin Harvick's victory as Earnhardt's replacement
- 2001: Dale Earnhardt Jr.'s victory in the summer race at Daytona
- 2004: Daytona 500

CHAPTER 1: 1895
THE FIRST RACE

The sport of stock car racing has a known beginning. Purists may argue when the first baseball game was played or even who came up with the rules. Or how golf was developed; when the initial football was picked up or who invented tennis.

There is no question about stock car racing or, for that matter, racing in general.

The first race between automobiles was held in France in 1894. Americans were introduced to the sport in 1895. There are no arguments about the timetable.

Frederick Upham Adams, an American mechanical engineer who invented the electric light pole, was struck by the attention given the 1894 marathon race in France. He was there to report on the race for the *Chicago Times-Herald* and recruited the paper's publisher Herman K. Kohlsaat to put up $5,000 in prize money plus a gold medal for a race in Chicago. Kohlstaat wasn't enamored with the idea, but agreed as long as Adams handled all the details.

Financially set, Adams then plotted out a 92 mile course from Chicago's Jackson Park to Waukegan, Illinois and back. He didn't consider a shorter race. Manufacturers wanted to prove durability. Speed wasn't that important, not with only a handful of passable roads in the whole country and few cars on them.

In a 16-month campaign, Adams toured the United States to find inventors and car builders willing to compete. His encouragement soared to new heights when the press of the nation featured the results of the Paris-Bordeau race in June 1895, explained author Peter Helck in his book *The Checkered Flag.*

French writers coined the term "automobile" to describe the horseless carriage. Adams ran a $500 contest through the *Chicago Times-Herald* to come up with an American name for them. Three entrants chose "motocycle," which was declared the winner although the term never really caught on.

Adams even rented a vacant storefront to store the 14 motocycles that inventors shipped to Chicago for the race. To participate in the race, motocycles were required to have a minimum of three wheels and be able to carry at least two people, one of whom was to be an umpire selected by the judges to ride with the driver during the race. Participants also had to run their vehicles through a preliminary test using equipment Adams obtained from Purdue University. The cars were placed on a machine that simulated road conditions. Developed by the Chicago City Railroad Company, the contraption measured various aspects of the performance, including fuel consumption and load capacity. The results were compared against a horse-drawn wagon. The cars won.

Adams then brought Kohlsaat to see the cars. The publisher was thrilled and eager for the race to start. The race was scheduled for July 4, an ambitious undertaking considering that only two or three people in the whole country were manufacturing cars at the time. The cars in storage never moved as no one submitted an entry form by July 3. Kohlsaat was embarrassed, but Adams rescheduled the race for November 2. However, that race never took place as only a handful of cars showed up. Adams compromised and the vehicles compete in what he called a "consolation" race for a $500 prize.

Only two cars actually were capable of competing. One, an import created by the Benz Co. and driven by Oscar Mueller, son of the vehicle's owner, featured a single-cylinder gasoline engine and a belt drive. Seats were arranged in the European style: drivers and passengers faced each other. The second car was constructed piecemeal by J. Frank and Charles Duryea, who had been born in Illinois but now ran a shop in Massachusetts. It came equipped with wooden wheels covered by pneumatic tires, a two-cylinder engine and a drive chain. The engine was covered by a bustle, which was popular in the early years of car manufacturing.

Years later, J. Frank Duryea wrote down his memories of that vehicle:

I now started with draughtsmen on plans for a new car, of which I had, from time to time, been making rough sketches during the past summer. But my work was interrupted by the necessity of preparing the old car for the race promoted by H. H. Kohlsaat of the Chicago Times-Herald. This race was set for November 2, and as driver, the Company sent me out to Chicago with the car on that date. Only the Mueller Benz and the Duryea cars were ready to start, so the race was postponed to Thanksgiving Day, November 28, 1895.

Duryea forgot to mention that when he and Mueller set off in the consolation race, they passed a farmer on a hay wagon. Initiating a long tradition, the farmer signaled one way with his hand and turned the other, right into Duryea's path. To avoid a collision, Duryea swerved into a ditch. The car had to be shipped back to Massachusetts for repairs.

Mueller eventually completed the 92 miles to Waukegan and back at a rate of 10 miles per hour.

That definitely encouraged Adams, who remained optimistic that enough competitors would arrive for the real race on Thanksgiving. After all, when he had announced the initial event, he received hundreds of application, but most came from individuals with high hopes and no cars. Adams shortened the race length to 54 miles, starting at Midway Plaisance and Jackson Park to Evanston and back.

Then, three days before the race, Chicago was hit by a blizzard. High, wind-blown drifts dotted the thoroughfares. The railroads ceased running. Even horses were kept in the barn. Nevertheless, eleven drivers gave Adams written pledges to show up. He couldn't expect to hold a race if they reneged. Kohlstaat was already being ridiculed by the rival *Tribune* and was unwilling to be humiliated by another cancellation.

Despite promises, only six vehicles chugged into Jackson Park on the appointed day. Some arrived late. Two were carried by horse-drawn drays. Working long hours, the Duryeas managed to repair their car and made it to the starting line, too.

After becoming a mechanic, Charles, the oldest of the brothers, found a job in Washington, D. C., in the growing bicycle industry. In 1889, J. Frank, fresh from high school, joined his brother. Charles recalled riding on their first horseless carriage that summer, an electric trolley that ran between Washington and Baltimore. They soon moved to Chicopee, Massachusetts to run their own bicycle company.

Charles, however, was drawn to gasoline-powered carriages. Depending on the source, he either read a magazine article about Carl Benz' engine in Germany and started duplicating it or was motivated to continue his own experiments after seeing the story. There's no way to completely sort fact from fiction. Charles was big on self-promoting, and his version of history changed from one reporter to another.

J. Frank eventually drew up the plans for a car, and, in 1893, the first Duryea took its initial test run. The tryout was witnessed by Erwin Markham, an investor in the project; Howard Bemis, who owned the farm where the maiden trip took place; and Rudy McPhee, a reporter for the *Springfield Evening-Union*. Duryea clearly had learned early about the power of publicity. J. Frank steered, while the witnesses pushed the carriage until the motor sputtered into operation.

With top speeds of 5 mph, the vehicle was powered by a one-cylinder engine with a three-speed transmission and a loose jacket ignition. It initially covered 25 feet before stalling. The next try measured 200 feet, halted only when the vehicle bumped into a pile of dirt. [1]

Everyone involved was said to be pleased with the results.

The car was very simple, with a single-cylinder, gasoline-fueled, water-cooled engine mounted horizontally under the carriage body. Friction drive transferred the power to the wheels. Top speed was about 7.5 miles per hour.

The brothers made some upgrades from their test model, including adding a two-cylinder engine, three-speed belt transmission, a throttle to control speed, and pneumatic tires. Then, the brothers saw an announcement in the local newspaper promoting the Chicago race and including an entry form. The Duryeas applied immediately.

They had five competitors on Thanksgiving Day. Of those, four were also piloting gasoline-driven vehicles: Frederick Haas in a De la Vergne-Benz; Mueller in his Benz; and Jerry O'Connor in a Benz sponsored by R. H. Macy, the department store. Mueller had replaced his car engine with a new one.

Two electric cars also putt-putted to the starting line. Henry Morris in an Electrobat and Harold Sturges in a two-ton car that bore his name. Neither was likely to win and considered the event an exhibition. Relay stations had been set up along the route with gasoline and ice to cool the engines, but there was no place available to recharge the batteries on the electric cars. And, they did not have enough power to complete the course. Neither did. They both drove to Lincoln Park and had to be towed back by horses.

Five were ready to go at the appointed time. Hampered by the weather, Mueller didn't get to the starting line until more than an hour after the race began.

An estimated 1,000 people turned out in overcoats and scarves stood near the start/finish line to watch the racers plod through Jackson Park where the University of Michigan was playing the University of Chicago in a football game. The official starting point was at 55th Street, then went to Michigan Avenue, on to Evansville and back again. President Grover Cleveland felt so strongly about the future of the horseless carriage that he asked the War Department to oversee the event.

Reporters were there, too, but either on foot or horseback.

"At 8:55 a.m., with an ear-muffed chilled population shuffling chilled feet for vantage points, Judge Kimball, watch in hand, gave the starting signal," Helck wrote.

J. Frank Duryea, who drew the front position, drove off first with independent observer Arthur W. White beside him. Duryea steered with a lever; steering wheels were still two years in the future. The car that was driven that day now sits proudly in the Smithsonian Institute. It was the only car in the Chicago race to rely on the pneumatic tires invented by Michelin, gaining traction in snow that wood or cloth tires couldn't match. It also had no trouble starting in the cold and chugged into the lead as spectators huddled together at the start/finish line gave a resounding cheer.

Charles Duryea, wrapped in furs, followed in a horse-drawn carriage along with members of the media.

Each car followed Duryea's lead in staggered intervals. Haas in a De la Vergne-Benz went off second. Fans in Jackson Park enjoying the football game cheered the drivers motoring past.

Some pitched in to free any car caught up in a snowdrift. That didn't help the De la Vergne Benz, which got mired in the slush between Jackson Park and 55th Street and had to withdraw after just two miles.

The Macy Benz rolled off third and quickly ran into trouble. It slid into a horse-drawn carriage then crossing the Pennsylvania railroad track. Driver Jerry O'Connor then "collided with an overturned sleigh that had just dumped its contents, including a *Times-Herald* reporter, into the snow," according to a report on the race written by Arthur R. Buchroch, in his 1974 book, *American Automobile Racing*.

Kohlstaat watched the race from the warmth of his Lake Shore Drive mansion. Promoter Adams later said his most vivid recollection was the publisher's "childish delight" while surveying the cars plowing through snowdrifts on the street below.

Duryea was leading until the steering gear broke. He lost 55 minutes for repairs. According to the official report from Judge Charles King, "Driver J. Frank Duryea had igniter trouble and located a tinsmith shop which was closed because of the holiday; went to the owner's home and got him out of bed to open the shop where he lighted the fire in the tinner's charcoal stove and forged out the igniter, and, after a delay of 55 minutes, according to his Umpire, Arthur White, he resumed the race at 3.20 pm."

Taking advantage, O'Connor had his car in front by the time the drivers reached Evanston despite running into a street car. Then he rammed into a carriage and gave up. Amid all the confusion, Duryea was able to move in front — a process that caused hat waving and cheers when he passed the Macy's damaged Benz in front of some of the 10,000 people who lined the route.

Behind him, Mueller was desperately trying to catch up. A third observer, Charlie Reid, was removed from the car after 35 miles, overcome by the cold and exposure in the open seats. After all, these cars were closer to motorcycles than modern sedans. Only an hour from the finish line (maybe 8 miles), Mueller, too, succumbed to the brutal weather. Umpire Charles Brady King left the warmth of his trailing horse-drawn carriage to hold onto Mueller and drive to keep the car in the race. King would go on to greater racing fame than Mueller: in 1895, he drove the first car in Detroit and then founded the world's first automobile club, the American Motor League, that same year. Later, he began building his own cars.

Duryea recorded the race in his memoir.

While still in the lead, the left front wheel struck a bad rut at such an angle that the steering arm was broken off. This arm had been threaded and screwed firmly to a shoulder, and it was a problem to extract the broken-off threaded part of the arm. When this was finally accomplished, we, fortunately, located a blacksmith shop where we forged down, threaded and replaced the arm.

While thus delayed, the Macy Benz passed us and held the lead as far as Evanston, where we regained it.

Having made the turn at Evanston, elated at being in the lead again, we started on the home trip. We had not yet come to Humboldt Park when one of the two cylinders ceased firing … This repair was completed in fifty-five minutes and we got going, feeling that the Macy Benz must surely be ahead of us, but learned later that the Macy did not get that far. Breaking the way through the snow in Humboldt and Garfield Parks furnished heavy work for the motor, but also indicated that all competitors were behind us.

After a stop for gasoline, and a four-minute wait for a passing train at a railroad crossing, we continued on to the finish in Jackson Park, arriving at 7:18 P.M.

The motor had at all times shown ample power, and at no time were we compelled to get out and push.

Duryea endured a series of delays, all carefully recorded: "2 minutes to oil engine; 8.5 minutes to tighten belt; one-half minute, right chain off; 6 minutes to bend clutch." The drivers also had to pause occasionally to let the Cottage Grove Horse Cars go by.

Chicago policemen hurried ahead of the slow-moving cars to keep the roads clear as possible. However, all along the route, bored children, tired of waiting for one of the cars to struggle by, started snowball fights. Police were unable to calm the melee, as the snowstorm had silenced all telephone and alarm boxes.

Perhaps 50 people were still waiting in the dark and cold 10.5 hours when, after starting, an exhausted J. Frank Duryea climbed down from his vehicle to claim the $2,000 first prize. His average speed was either slightly above 5 mph for the full race or close to 7.5 mph when repair time is excluded. He had spent more than 7 hours and 53 minutes on the road battling the conditions and another 2 hours and 30 minutes fixing the resulting damage.

King finished 24 minutes later, driving with one hand on the tiller and the other grasping the unconscious car owner. Had Mueller gotten to the starting line on time, Duryea would only have been a footnote in history.

Instead, on December 5 — not explanation was given for the week-long delay between the race and the awards ceremony — Duryea received his check. The judges decided to honor all the participants. Among other handouts, Mueller was awarded $1,500 for "performance and economy of operation," Buchroch said. For inexplicable reasons, the gold medal went to the Electrobat. Maybe there was no prize money left.

Duryea spoke at the awards ceremony and claimed to have built the car by himself with the aid of a couple of assistants. He did not mention his bother, Charles, precipitating a feud that grew worse in time.

Publisher Kohlsaat did not care about the sibling rivalry. He was thrilled with the results. "Persons who are inclined … to decry the development of the horseless carriage ... will be forced to recognize it as an admitted mechanical achievement, highly adapted to the most urgent needs of our civilization," his newspaper opined the day after the race.

Duryea invested the prize money in his fledgling automobile company, which had actually been incorporated eight months prior to the race.

In March, 1896, the first commercial American automobile, the Duryea motor wagon, hit the streets. Two months later, New York City motorist Henry Wells banged into a bicyclist with his new Duryea. The rider suffered a broken leg. Wells was arrested and spent a night in jail after the nation's inaugural traffic accident.

The Chicago victory made the Duryea famous. J. Frank went on to win the next two American races — in New York City in 1896 where Charles came in second; and in Providence, Rhode Island in 1899 — and then one in England.

Meanwhile, his brother was promoting himself as the true driver of the car used in Chicago. He also claimed to have designed the car. Actually, according to J. Frank Duryea's biography, he contributed a steering lever. Charles supposedly didn't even see the car until his brother gave him a test drive.

Charles' extravagant claims acerbated the split between the brothers, who never reconciled. Their company built both 3- and 4-wheelers, but was dissolved in 1898. J. Frank then joined the Stevens Arms and Tool Company in Massachusetts, which produced the Stevens-Duryea vehicle through 1927. Charles moved to Pennsylvania and became involved with several unsuccessful ventures to build cars. He eventually became the mechanical editor and consulting engineer for the *Automobile Trade Journal* until his death in 1939 at age 76.

The question over the identity of the actual winning Chicago race driver lingered until 1945, almost seven years after Charles died. A committee headed by Captain Eddie Rickenbacker finally certified J. Frank Duryea's premier role in American motor sports.

At age 89, the venerable racer took part in a 1959 New York automobile event in New York City. He died eight years later, fully aware of his important role in automotive history.

"When I began work upon the horseless carriage back in 1892, no one could see what the automobile would mean to my fellow beings in peace or in war," Duryea said in 1942. "And, yet, the automobile to this very day contains not a few of the fundamental features which I was the first to devise, design, build, or order built to my specifications."

About 30 years after Duryea died, Chicago immortalized him on a piece of granite marking the starting point of America's first auto race. Today, that site is located on a small grassy strip in the middle of a busy intersection.

There, early every Thanksgiving morning since the late 1990s, over a century after J. Frank Duryea chugged down a snow-covered road into history, several hundred motor sports enthusiasts have been gathering at what is now known affectionately as *The Rock* to pay tribute to him and to the other men who pioneered what is today one of the world's largest spectator sports.

Every element of the sport was visible that first day: harsh, dangerous conditions; timely pit stops; close competition and camaraderie among the participants; fans eager to watch a race; cars; and the determination to win regardless of circumstances.

Every ounce of that grit would be necessary for the sport to endure the coming decades. The curves in the road faced by auto racing were about to get worse than a few snowdrifts.

CARS IN AMERICA: EARLY PROTOTYPES

Cars had been around long before six of them showed up in a snowy Chicago morning in 1895 to compete.

In 1769, Nicolas Joseph Cugnot of France built the first steam-power car. Its primary status is recognized by the British Royal Automobile Club and the Automobile Club de France.

Almost 60 years later, April 1, 1826, Samuel Morey (1762-1843) filed a patent, bearing the signatures of John Quincy Adams and Henry Clay, for an internal combustion engine. A Connecticut native, Morey accumulated 20 patents, mostly related to steamboats. Other inventors, including George Brayton, Stephanie Reese, Henry Nadig and Wallis Harris, all of whom produced self-propelled machines. In 1872, Brayton patented his hot-air engine, which became the basis for gas turbine engines.

The gasoline engine appeared in 1876 when German engineer Nikolaus August Otto invented and later patented a successful four-stroke engine, known as the "Otto cycle." He promptly installed it on a motorcycle.

In 1879, a New York-based Civil War veteran and attorney applied for the patent for a combustion-powered engine. George Selden may have been motivated by a hoof-and-mouth outbreak that devastated horses used by the Rochester street railway. He actually had no intention of building his "road engine," which looks like a bicycle with a seat and a 37-lb motor attached to the front wheel. Selden enclosed the engine's crankcase and, along with other improvements, was able to produce two horsepower.

George Selden (right, standing) and his sons.

Selden delayed as long as possible before submitting the final paperwork for his patent. While he dithered, Elwood Haynes, a Kokomo, Indiana field superintendent with a natural gas company, put together a one-cylinder water-cooled engine with a carriage. Haynes was simply trying to ease the strain on horses during his long trips.

In 1894, he tried out his little buggy. It worked, and Haynes began to use it during his job. His feat was recognized 28 years later on the site of his first test. A plaque there calls the landmark "the birthplace of a new era of transportation, the nucleus and the beginning of the gigantic automobile industry."

Haynes was quickly forgotten, because Selden finally received his long-delayed patent November 5, 1895, less than a month before the initial American race and a year after the first automobile race. However, Selden identified Brayton's 2-cycle engine as an important component of his invention. That admission did not initially affect his rights. During the next eight years, the New York attorney earned about $200,000 by licensing his engine for use by car manufacturers.

Meanwhile, Europeans were keeping busy with their own efforts. In 1894 Count Philipe Albert de Dion de Malfiance won a race on a 78.75 mile road course between Paris and Rouen in France, driving at an average of about 11.6 mph. Some 19 cars participated in the event, which drew international attention. Reportedly, to signal the end of the race, someone grabbed a checkered tablecloth and waved it, initiating that tradition, although the origin of the checkered flag has never been documented.

Count de Dion drove a 20-horsepower steam tractor, which hauled an open Victorian "industrial vehicle" and split the prize money with second-place Peugeot, which looked more like a car and, they said, "was more desirable for social reasons."

A year later, Emile Levassor won the first marathon race, averaging 15 mph on solid tires for the 740-mile French jaunt between Paris and Bordeaux. Levassor, a woodworker, is credited with developing the first real transmission. He also moved the engine to the front of the vehicle and added rear-wheel drive. He did not survive long enough to enjoy his innovations. He was killed during a Paris to Marseille race in 1897.

Count de Dion motored on, despite family objections that he would squander his inheritance. In 1882, he joined the maker Georges Bouton and later with Bouton's brother-in-law Charles-Armand Trepardoux to form a French company to manufacture what they labeled "velocipedes." The term "automobile" came later. They came up with a three-wheeler. The company's first car was steam driven with the boiler placed midway on the vehicle.

The first four-wheel De Dion-Bouton car, the "Vis-a'-vis,"

Count Philipe Albert de Dion de Malfiance

was introduced in 1899, and more than 1,500 were sold by 1901. In 1902, the engine was moved to the front. A whole series of engines and vehicles then followed, making De Dion Bouton one of the most important car manufacturers in the world.

The Count's main rival was the Mercedes, developed by German Karl Friedrich Benz. In 1871, he founded his first company with partner August Ritter to supply building materials. Looking for another source of income, Benz began work in a gasoline engine and received his first patent in 1879. In 1883, he founded Benz & Company to produce industrial engines. His first car was driven in 1885, and a few months after, he received a patent for his gas-fueled automobile. In July, 1886, the first Benz went on sale. In 1893, the Benz Velo became the world's first inexpensive, mass-produced car, an irony considering the hefty price tag on Mercedes-Benz cars today.

Henry Ford wanted to follow that business model and founded his own automobile company in 1903 after winning a match race against Alexander Winton. He didn't have much money, so ignored the Selden patent. Naturally, Selden sued. Ford lost the resulting lawsuit in 1909, but doubled his sales as publicity from the legal wrangling kept his name and cars in the public eye. He also refused to pay Selden a penny. An appeals court eventually reversed the original ruling, finding that Selden's patent specified a Brayton 2-cycle engine while Ford was using the Otto 4-cycle engine.

Selden's patent was broken.

Freed from the financial noose, a variety of entrepreneurs began manufacturing cars. According to a Wall Street Journal on-line account, as many as 2,600 vehicle-making companies have been started in the U.S. since 1896, when the Duryea brothers launched Duryea Motor Wagon Co. in Springfield, Massachusetts.

"Some never really got off the ground, or made only one car," reported Mark Patrick, curator of the National Automotive History Collection at the Detroit Public Library.

Most of these companies were formed before 1929 and fell victim to the Great Depression. Others were bought out, merged or simply faded into history. Today, only the Ford Motor Company remains from all the original companies that put America on the road and set the horse out to pasture.

CHAPTER 2: 1938

THE ARRIVAL OF BILL FRANCE

Many historians look to 1936 as the key year in the arrival of stock car racing as a sport. They highlight the first, formal stock car race held on the sands of Daytona Beach, which quickly established the community as a base for the sport and attracted widespread publicity. Reporters were drawn by the glittering array of drivers who competed for a hefty $5,000 purse and by the unusual combination beach\paved venue. Actually, the race was only important for Daytona Beach and was a financial failure, forcing the city to back away from promoting a second race. The 1937 version was sponsored by the Elks Club, which also lost money and interest in racing simultaneously.

That led to 1938 and the two races that may have been the most important in the history of stock car racing. One introduced the man who would lead the sport into the spotlight. The other set the standards that would eventually pull stock car racing from its rough-and-tumble origins into legitimacy.

No one could have foreseen what those races meant. After all, stock car racing as a sport did not exist in 1938. Tracks speckled the landscape, but featured smaller versions of Indy-like cars. Occasional stock car races were held at various fairgrounds and the like, where local drivers kicked up dirt on makeshift tracks.

Promoters thought that family cars on the track would induce residents caught up in the Depression to part with a few extra pennies. None of the events organized into any kind of official series, which was hardly a new development in this arena. Some historians even date the beginning of the sport back to rumrunners who were part of the Whiskey Rebellion in the late 1700s, when farmers upset with a new tax simply began to hide their stills from revenuers. Their efforts were boosted by Prohibition in the 1920s and unaffected by repeal of the 18th amendment in the early 1930s because of the taxes placed on alcohol.

That kind of background guaranteed that stock cars drivers emerging from the rural backwoods of North Carolina, South Carolina, Georgia and Tennessee were, at best, unsavory. After all, most were involved in illegally transporting alcohol from unregulated stills to Atlanta — Highway 421 was a popular route — and bringing back the empties. Naturally, they had to outrun federal agents through one-lane, unlit rural roads. That required "souped-up" cars.

Famed mechanic Red Vogt recalled building patrol cars for police on one side of his Atlanta garage while the other side was reserved for even faster "liquor cars" for bootleggers.

The men who drove those special creations were not interested in oval tracks, but preferred the dirt byways of the rural South. In the 1930s, a few boastful drivers gathered on a farm in Stockbridge, Georgia, and lined up, door-handle to door-handle, "slamming and banging" against each other with an audience of maybe 50 spectators. The next Sunday, about 100 people showed up.

"When thousands began lining up to get a chance to watch the race, the farmer fenced off the pasture, put up a gate and charged admission," Robert Hagstrom wrote in *The NASCAR Way*. This wasn't a sport by any definition, but more of a violent hobby.

There was no evident public interest anyway. After the initial rush in 1895, when hand-built cars careened haphazardly through Chicago's snow-covered streets, manufacturers had become more organized and began to produce two lines of vehicles. Street cars, like the Oldsmobile and Cord, were fine for the everyday driver willing to brave the rough roads and the occasional collision with a horse or pedestrian. Race cars, however, were meant for the track, and grew sleeker and less familiar as time passed.

In Ormond Beach, the small resort community seven miles north of Daytona Beach, and the home of stock car races on its increasingly famous shoreline from 1903 to 1910, stopped attracting family cars and became deluged by vehicles that would never need to find a parking space on a city street.

As stock car racing continued in a muted, disreputable fashion, the focus of automobile racing in those years centered on a 328-acre tract in Indiana, a state then home to an array of car builders. In 1909, four entrepreneurs converted a rich Indiana stretch of farmland into a track designed for manufacturers as a place to test their vehicles. One of them, Carl Fisher, owned a local car company called Prest-O-Lite.

The track, which opened in August that year, was then located five miles northwest of the Hoosier state capital, but has since been swallowed up by development. The 2.5-mile track was created in symmetrical design with two straightaways and four, 440-yard turns, each lightly banked at nine degrees. In contrast, Daytona International Speedway is banked at 31 degrees. The owners opted for a surface of crushed rock and tar, which turned out to be slippery and created havoc for the first drivers. So, "3,200,000 paving bricks were imported by rail from the western part of the state in the fall, laid on their sides in a bed of sand and fixed with mortar." [1] From that point on, Indianapolis Motor Speedway has been known as "The Brickyard."

A quartet, Fisher, James Allison, Frank Wheeler and Arthur

Newby, occasionally set up races on the track and featured some of the cars available in the local showrooms. Unfortunately for their bank accounts, the idea of watching cars test against each other failed to excite local residents despite three, three-day events, so, after a dismal 1910, the owners decided to pour their money into a one-day extravaganza on Memorial Day 1911. They selected 500 miles as the ultimate endurance test. To make sure the top drivers came, they created a $14,250 first prize. The Indianapolis 500 was born and would remain racing's premier event until finally being surpassed by the Daytona 500 in the 1990s.

Cars competing in the Indianapolis 500 became increasingly aerodynamic and far removed from the lumpy, creaky automobiles that the average driver could pick up at his dealer. They zoomed around the track at vastly higher speeds, too. Their pilots, men like Barney Oldfield and Ralph DePalma, became the epitome of the country's racing and inspired the dreams of little boys with motor oil in their veins.

When the competitors — who risked their lives each time they turned on the ignition — weren't concentrating on the single, annual race in Indiana; they came to Daytona Beach in an effort to set the world speed record on the unusual, nearly flat, quartz-imbued sand. From 1911 to 1935, a collection of single-built complex speedsters from around the world, including Baltimore-born Irishman Henry O'Neal de hane Segrave, Englishman Malcolm Campbell, and Americans Ray Keech and Frank Lockhart, who journeyed to east-central Florida to test their courage and luck on the shoreline. Of those, only Campbell died in bed.

For Daytona Beach, at the time only a small resort community, the occasional publicity from the attempts to set a world-speed record was a godsend. The city happily underwrote the expenses of drivers taking timed runs though the measured mile. Only Campbell, who made his millions in libel insurance and didn't need financial support, paid his own way.

In 1935, after Campbell was lured back by city officials for one last effort, the good times stopped. The English businessman averaged a then-record 276.82 miles per hour and decided that the elusive 300 mph mark would have to be achieved someplace else. City fathers panicked. How were they going to draw tourists to fill their rickety motels and fuel their tourist-based economy?

The answer, they concluded after much debate, was stock car racing. In 1936, like Indianapolis, they posted a large purse ($5,000) and invited the top competitors in the country to east-central Florida for a 250-mile race in March. It would be a warm-up for the annual Indianapolis 500 on Memorial Day. Then, they entrusted Sig Haugdahl to develop a track.

The diminutive Norwegian had immigrated first to Minnesota in 1910 and then to Florida a decade later. After racing motorcycles for awhile, he shifted to cars. In 1922, Haugdahl joined the quest for speed on Daytona Beach's hard sand, becoming the first driver to top 180 mph. His record didn't receive any national recognition because he was not a member of the American Automobile Association, the official sanctioning body. Haugdahl retired from racing in 1934, but was the perfect choice to lay out the course. He asked his friend, Bill France, to help him. It was a fateful decision.

In an era when adult men averaged about 5'6", William Henry Getty France really stood out. A giant at 6'5" tall, he eventually towered over a sport that was little more than a disorganized weekend avocation for a bunch of moonshine runners. Without him, stock car racing doesn't get a green flag and never powers into the nation's living rooms.

Haugdahl and France chose to run their makeshift, 3.2-mile track along the beach and then onto a paved road that paralleled the shoreline. The unusual course worked only because a community-minded owner allowed them to cut the south turn through the dunes.

The race had to be different than Indianapolis, so the city opened it to regular cars, not the hotrods rocketing around The Brickyard. The novel idea immediately attracted media attention and public interest. Many of the drivers regularly competed in the Indianapolis 500.[2] Fords dominated the 27-car starting lineup, but there was an Oldsmobile, Chevrolet, Auburn, Zephyr and Willys represented as well. The American Automobile Association sanctioned the race; fans flocked to the beach, but the event was a financial and competitive disaster.

Deep ruts formed in the dunes; the tide rolled in early. Lighter cars got stuck. Heavier cars simply clogged with sand. Every car in the field had to be towed at least twice. No one really knew who won, least of all AAA officials who simply picked Milt Marion, a dirt-track driver from Long Island, and award him the $1,700 first prize. Two drivers quickly filed protests, but any complaints were immediately dismissed.

Trapped in the midst of the Great Depression, the city lost an estimated $22,000 and refused to sponsor another race.

Stock car racing looked to be dead. That's when France stepped in. "Big Bill" was born in Washington, D.C. (although some sources say Virginia) in 1909 and was the son of a teller at Park Savings Bank in the nation's capital. France would demonstrate a skill with figures later on, but, early in life, he simply was attracted to automobiles. He often stayed home from school and impetuously took the family Model-T Ford for a few spins around a high-banked board track in nearby Laurel, Maryland. Eventually, he decided to become a mechanic. Supposedly, his early success was assured when he would get up early on wintry mornings to crank cars for Washington bureaucrats. He would have had plenty of work. Hand cracks, needed to start cars that relied on magnetos for power instead of batteries, did not fall completely out of favor until 1935.

He may have been busy through the 1920s, but The Depression hit him hard. Most people couldn't even afford a car, ending income from cranking engines. Discouraged by a deep snowfall in 1934, France decided to head for a warmer climate in hopes of improving his economic situation. He emptied his bank account of his life savings, $75. Then, he, his wife, Anne, a former nurse, and young son, Bill, climbed into their Hupmobile, tied a trailer to the bumper and headed south. He picked up cash along the way by repairing cars of stranded motorists making the same trek.[3]

Anne reportedly had relatives in New Smyrna Beach, which is located about 15 miles south of Daytona Beach, although Bill France Jr.* denied that claim years later.

Bill France Sr. later said the family was actually going to Miami, but he grew instantly enamored with the beautiful beach in Daytona and the inviting waters of the Atlantic Ocean.

"We drove across the Ormond Bridge and out onto the beach," France recalled in 1970. "The tide was out, and I remember looking down the beach and seeing the tide for the first time. It was a beautiful fall day, and there wasn't a soul on the beach." He drove south on the hard-packed sand to the Main Street Pier. "We changed into our swimming trunks in the trailer and went swimming."

One dip in the warm, salty water was enough for France. "I just liked Daytona," he continued, "and we decided it was where we wanted to be."

He also recalled newspaper accounts about Campbell and the chase for the land-speed record. One day, France would own the car he saw speeding to a land-speed record in 1935.

---

* Bill France's son, Bill, has been called Junior for decades, but that's for convenience sake. He has a different middle name, Clifton, but writers needed some way to distinguish between the two men.

After a few days, he found a job with a local car dealer and settled down. A year later, France bought an Amoco gas station and joined Haugdahl to design the Beach-Road Course. He also drove in the first Daytona Beach race, finishing fifth.

When the city decided not to sponsor a race in 1937, France joined with Haugdahl to convince the local Elks Club to put up the cash for a second try. The fraternal organization coughed up $100. That kind of money naturally was not much inducement to the nation's top drivers, so only local drivers participated. The race was moved to Labor Day in hopes of getting a holiday crowd. The temporary stands were full along the dunes. C.D. "Smoky" Purser, who owned the local New York Bar & Grill, came home first and earned $43.57.

Despite the crowd, the race still lost money — not as much as the year before, but enough to convince the Elks to bow their antlers and walk away. Haugdahl, too, threw up his hands and retired from the promoting business. City Council decided to contact an outside promoter, Ralph Hankinson, who was well known for his work with Sprint cars and Midgets. Hankinson told them the cost would be $20,000 to put on a first-class event. That was too rich for Daytona Beach officials, who began considering other options. Purser, too, said he was willing to sponsor the race if other local companies chipped in. Tepid response forced him to back off the idea.

France was not ready to give up. He decided to hold a July 4 race in 1938, regardless of outside assistance. With the action, stock car racing was born as a sport.

His first step was to enlist Charlie Reese, a local restaurant owner and a friend, to put up $1,000 in prize money as long as France did the grunt work. Reese was not a disinterested bystander. He was owner and president of the Daytona Beach Racing Association, which France formed as a route to convince local businesses to chip in a few rewards for lap leaders. Reese was also the media source for information about the races. In published newspaper stories, he described the new grandstands, the addition of a public address announcer and other details. France was not mentioned.

Nevertheless, France was very active, although his scrounging for prizes was not overwhelming: "a box of 'Hav-A-Tampa' cigars, a case of Pennzoil motor oil, a pair of sunglasses from Walgreen's, two cases of Pabst Blue Ribbon beer, a bottle of rum, a $2.50 credit at the local men's clothing store and a $25 credit towards any automobile purchased from Dick Rose's used car lot." [4]

Having no experience promoting a race, France was reluctant to take on the task and drive at the same time. He tried to call Hankinson, who lived in Orange City about 20 miles outside Daytona Beach. Hankinson, who was inducted into the National Sprint Car Hall of Fame when it opened in 1990, had gotten into the business in the Midwest by convincing various fair boards that "auto racing was a cheap, yet profitable form of entertainment in the Depression Era." [5]

The hotel, still located at 300 South Volusia Avenue, once hosted race drivers from Hankinson's racing circuit who wintered in the area.

Hankinson declined to accept a collect call from France, who reluctantly decided to promote the race himself. Hankinson would later try to horn into France's promotion in Daytona Beach, but would be rebuffed by City Council. In the early 1940s, Hankinson also tried to ban France from competing in races that Hankinson promoted. That effort failed because France, who had emerged as a top driver, was too popular with fans.

From the moment France became a promoter, he broke with tradition. He was well aware race promoters had the awful reputation for cheating both fans and drivers by broadcasting unfounded claims of large purses and famous participants to draw crowds. At the same time, France realized drivers wouldn't hesitate to cheat. After all, most still were illegally transporting liquor away from any track and had developed untested techniques for enhancing their engine's ability to outrun federal agents.

As a driver, France had been burned by fake promotions and was resolved to counter the problem. Any announced purse at his races would be accurate and, more importantly to the drivers, actually paid. In addition, he created a series of rules to be sure the cars were as equal as possible. In 1938, several cars underwent pre-race inspections. After the race, cars that finished in the top five positions underwent detailed inspections in what is now known as the Armory on Ballough Road.

He didn't ask drivers for advice about inspections. He simply ordered them. There were no arguments — not with France.

Long-time associate Jim Hunter, a newspaperman who headed France's public relations efforts for decades, recalled many discussions with his late boss. "Bill always let you speak your piece," Hunter said. "And if you disagreed with him that was OK, if he thought you had a good reason. But, he had a way of looking at you over his glasses after a while, and, when he did that, you knew he'd had about enough of you. Bill France didn't lose many arguments." [6]

The first race France promoted was held July 10 after rain washed out the planned holiday event. France chose the date based on the tide tables, a necessity considering that the 1936 race ended abruptly as the ocean rolled ashore. Borrowing an idea from motorcycle racing, which had relocated from Atlanta to the beach in 1936, France had packed the dunes with marl, a natural clayey substance that hardened as it dried. He then posted thousands of posters in hopes of drawing an audience.

An estimated 4,000 to 5,000 people paid 50 cents each to

watch Ormond Beach fireman Danny Murphy in a 1938 Ford sponsored by a bar and grill took home the $300 first prize and $55 worth of assorted incentives posted by the local businesses. France finished right behind. Murphy may have won $300, but France and Reese made a small profit on the 47-lap race — reportedly $200, which didn't cover the time they invested, but enough to encourage them to host a second race on Labor Day.

This holiday race established the France style. Every car underwent a pre-race inspection. France ordered specifications from manufacturers and used them to verify that the cars were "strictly stock," a term that he would later use to describe his top race series in 1949. Later, he would call it the "Grand National" Division, borrowing a time-honored term from English horse racing. Every engine part was measured and calibrated, a necessary step that set a standard for post-race inspections.

He increased the distance of the race by two laps to 156.8 miles and charged drivers a $10 entry fee. In addition, beginning what would become an incessant drumbeat of publicity, France required drivers to participate in a holiday parade. He added a 42-foot high scoreboard, a loudspeaker and timing devises so spectators would know the speeds of the cars. He also charged $1 for a seat. Another 4,000 or so people showed up, much to France's delight. He and Reese would earn $1,100 apiece for this event, enough to ensure they would continue to promote races.

At 10:30 am, 14 cars headed down the beach at full throttle. Purser took the lead on lap 28 and scurried across the finish line for the victory. However, the local favorite did not hang around to collect his check. Instead, he drove by the reviewing stand and into Daytona Beach. What happened next is confusing, since several people claimed to follow Purser and found him busily make drastic changes to his engine.

One author insisted that France was the detective and found

Purser replacing cylinders in Roy Strange's garage. That's plausible, but unlikely, since the local newspaper didn't relate such a story, but simply reported that Purser came back to the track almost three hours later. Insisting he was not supposed to get his car inspected until three hours after the race, Purser said he had to stop at his restaurant before collecting the trophy.

Backed by a vote of the other drivers, France promptly disqualified him. As a result, Purser heads a list of distinguished (and not-so-distinguished) drivers who would be disqualified for failing to live up to standards that France established.

France's action created a dilemma: France had actually finished second. As a result of the disqualification, he then became the winner of his own race. Reese didn't think that was a good idea. So, France declared Lloyd Moody, who was third, would claim the checkered flag. France accepted second-place money. The decision demonstrated that France was playing by different rules than other promoters. It established his credibility and credibility for any races he organized.

Later on, France raced occasionally with a pre-World War II team run by Raymond Parks, which featured legendary Georgia rumrunners Roy Hall and Lloyd Seay and was the first real team in stock car racing. In 1940, France won the national championship, a mythical title at a time when many drivers wore crowns handed out willy-nilly by unscrupulous promoters.

Racing suspended during World Warr II, but after the war ended, the sport resumed. Reportedly, France had a conversation with Wilton Garrison, then sports editor of the *Charlotte Observer*. According to MotorSportsNews.Net staff writer Robyn Snell, "Garrison informed Big Bill that he needed to create a series of races where the rules were always the same, week in, and week out and were consistently enforced. Garrison then proceeded to suggest to Big Bill that a points system needed to be established to determine an overall champion."

Snell is the only author to claim Garrison inspired NASCAR. Still, it's plausible. The idea had to come from somewhere. Of course, France could have done it without Garrison's suggestion. After all, he had run several organizations since 1938. In 1946, France set up the National Championship Stock Car Circuit, which he operated out of his Daytona Beach home. Atlanta's Fonty Flock, one of three racing brothers, took home the first NCSCC championship and a $3,000 check. The fact Flock actually received any money confirmed France's reputation for honesty. Promoters before and after the war were considered unscrupulous and more likely to abscond with any of the proceeds than to share them with competitors.

Moreover, France recognized the need for national standards. Still reluctant to run everything himself, France asked the AAA for assistance, but, as with Hankinson, was turned down. Snell said the AAA wanted nothing to do with "a bunch of red-neck rabble of jalopy drivers."

So, in December 1947, France called a meeting of about 35 race promoters and created the National Association of Stock Car Auto Racing (NASCAR), now the largest and most powerful racing organization in the country. He later built Daytona International Speedway, which rightly calls itself "The World Center of Racing."

Still, nothing France did could compare to his decision to host that race in 1938 when the sport was virtually moribund, when stock car racing was still on shifting sand. With France, it finally had someone with a vision and willingness to create a real sport and move it beyond just a weekend diversion for backwoods roughnecks.

"Big Bill France … put down the foundation for what became an unimagined success." [6]

CHAPTER 3: 1950
SUPERSPEEDWAYS JOIN NASCAR

There's nothing about Darlington, South Carolina that could possibly suggest the tiny community in the Pee Dee region somehow would play a major role in the survival of stock car racing. Located in Darlington County, the miniscule city held only 6,720 residents in 2000, according to the U.S. Census. That's even smaller than the 9,000 there in 1950, the year when Darlington Raceway opened. The whole county only has three cities of any size: Darlington, Lamar and Hartsville. Its only distinction prior to the racetrack was that David Rogerson Williams (1776-1830), governor and scientific experimenter, was a native of Darlington. His fame did not come from any of his political initiatives, but because he supposedly introduced the mule to Southern agriculture.

One more prominent resident deserves some credit. His name was Harold Brasington, a peanut farmer, construction company owner or businessman, depending on the source. One thing is certain: he wanted to build a racetrack on an old cotton and/or peanut field in his hometown.

The first stock car race at that track would begin the process of elevating the sport beyond its meager southern base. It may have been the most significant NASCAR race in history.

Brasington knew Bill France and even competed in the 1938 Beach-Road Course race. His inspiration did not come from Daytona Beach, but from Indianapolis, the center of racing at that time. Brasington had attended a race at Indianapolis — like everything in the usually undocumented history of racing, what particular race he attended varies based on who is telling the story; it was either 1933 or after the World War II — and came away overawed by the spectacle of thousands of people watching 33 cars lap the 2.5-mile track at more than 100 miles per hour.

He spoke to France, who was not interested in a paved facility in the middle of nowhere. "I told them that I didn't think a track in a little town like Darlington would go," France recalled years later.

Undaunted, Brasington tried to lure friends and family into the project with limited success. "Most folks around here thought Harold had lost his mind," said Harold King, a Darlington native who later spent 50 years as an employee of the raceway.

Nothing happened until after the war ended anyway. Military demands dried up available fuel and tires, so racing had stopped. Drivers, owners and promoters found work or went into combat. Bill France, for example, worked at the Daytona Beach Boat Works during the war. After Japan surrendered, he returned to racing and began promoting events in Georgia, and North and South Carolina. At best, the sport was chaotic and disorganized.

As Tim Flock, a Georgia moonshine hauler and a two-time NASCAR champion, once said, "We didn't have no tickets, no safety equipment, no fences, no nothing. Just a bunch of these bootleggers who'd been arguing all week about who had the fastest car." [1]

That's why France invited promoters, race car builders, top mechanics, lawyers and anyone else who might be interested, to a meeting in the Ebony Room of Daytona Beach's Streamline

Hotel, then the tallest structure in Daytona Beach — the hotel is still standing, looking something like a huge pie wedge. A new owner spent millions refurbishing it in 2015.

Together — estimates vary from 18 to 30 people — they formed NASCAR. France owned the room where the meeting took place, and, not surprisingly, was elected president. Within three years, he bought out other investors. NASCAR has remained controlled by the France family ever since.

France was not the only businessman with an idea to making money off stock car racing. Within a few months, NASCAR was competing for drivers, tracks and fans with the National Stock Car Racing Organization, the United States Stock Car Racing Association, the National Auto Racing League, and the American Stock Car Racing Association, among others.

To counter his opposition, France buttressed his reputation for fairness by arranging insurance for his usually insolvent drivers. That move alone helped draw the best-known competitors. He demonstrated his power by holding his first official NASCAR race in Charlotte, North Carolina, home of Olin Bruton Smith, then head of the National Stock Car Racing Association — and later the owner of Charlotte (now Lowe's) Motor Speedway, Texas Motor Speedway and Atlanta Motor Speedway, among others. Smith remains an adamant opponent of the France family and still talks of starting a rival circuit in an effort to undercut NASCAR. Old enmities die hard.

While France organized the sport, Brasington focused on his proposed track. He ignored advice from colleagues and, using a napkin, plotted out a 1.25-mile track He didn't own any site, but reportedly spoke to farmer Sherman Ramsey during a card game. Ramsey's grandson, Anthony Brown, said, during the game, Brasington asked Ramsey what he planned to do with the old DuBose Plantation. Ramsey had purchased the tract during the

Depression and said he considered letting tenant farmers use it.

Brasington suggested a track might be nice on the east end of the plantation, near Hartsville Road. Ramsey agreed. The two men didn't even shake hands, Brown recalled. Ramsey simply said "sure" and ordered the cards to be dealt, Brown told author Jim Hunter, a former president of the track and a long-time official with the International Speedway Corporation.

Ramsey was shrewd, however. He took stock instead of cash. Brasington probably didn't have much money to offer; he had borrowed all he could already.

Drawing on the Indianapolis model, Brasington imagined an elongated oval with two identical turns at either end. However, after returning from a business trip, Ramsey checked on the construction and insisted that an existing pond be left untouched. Brasington accommodated that request by redrawing his sketchy blueprints, creating an egg-shaped design with "the eastern end wide, sweeping and flat, and the western end narrow, tight and steeply banked." [2]

Over time, the pond became known as a "minnow" pond, and the pond still exists, located behind the Pearson Tower on the west side of the track.

Brasington, who was elected into the South Carolina Athletic Hall of Fame in 2001, was eager to get started. Soon after Ramsey grunted his okay, Brasington clambered into some earthmoving equipment — supposedly borrowed from his own business — and started haphazardly leveling the soil himself. He eventually had to work at nights after his wife received a complaint from a local Southern Baptist minister that all the weekend labor was desecrating the Sabbath.

As France would do in 1958 to build Daytona International Speedway, Brasington sold stock to raise money and worked long hours on the equipment. He apparently lacked sufficient funds to hire an architect.

"When Brasington was building (Turn 2) — and he was eye-balling it the whole way — it went a little wide, and he basically had to stop in the middle because they were getting right to the highway," Russell Branham, the track's publicist/historian/author, told columnist Bob Christ in 2001. "He had to come to a stop, come to a point, then come into the straightaway. So, when you're in Turn 2, you have to turn again in the same turn. They call it the toughest turn in NASCAR." [3]

It took a year to complete the track and pave it with asphalt. France was not impressed. His drivers had never competed on a track longer than a single mile; none had driven a race on asphalt. He doubted his cars could handle the strain and was concerned that an embarrassing showing would undermine what limited credibility his sport had.

As France hesitated, Brasington made a deal with the Mason Benner's Central States Racing Association (CSRA) to provide teams for a Labor Day race. At the same time, Sam Nunis, a Pennsylvania-based promoter who ran Atlanta's Lakewood Speed-way, was talking about hosting his own 500-mile race at the track, possibly over the July 4 weekend. Nunis had run a 150-miler on his track in October 1949 and drew an estimated 33,452 people, the largest crowd of the year. France had allowed his drivers to participate and was concerned that the cash generated by such a throng would give Nunis the muscle to pay bigger purses. He knew fully well NASCAR drivers would not hesitate to jump ship if the money was better elsewhere.

Caught in the middle, France still couldn't decide if he would support a Darlington race. Fortunately for him, Benner had a problem, too. He was unable to lure enough drivers to Darlington to make a decent field. He and France agreed to co-sanction the race. The history books call the race the 13th of the 1950 NASCAR season and the first NASCAR event on a superspeedway. But that's only half correct. Since the CSRA quickly faded into oblivion, it rarely gets a mention.

Unsure himself how stock cars could handle 500 miles, Nunis called off his proposed 150-miler and returned to sprint car promoting. France had the Labor Day holiday to himself and his stock cars, provided they could endure.

That holiday weekend was selected because it was the closest to the one-year anniversary of the Brasington-Ramsey agreement. Still, races are often held on holidays. The summer race at Daytona, for example, always runs on July 4 holiday weekend. Only Mother's Day and Easter were considered sacrosanct, so no races were ever scheduled on those days for decades. The first Mother's Day race in NASCAR history occurred in 2005.

In keeping with the Indianapolis tradition, and to allow more time for publicity, Brasington scheduled two weeks of qualifying for his weekend race. Curtis Turner won the pole with a record speed of 82.04 mph, even though Wally Campbell, who started 60th, actually posted a slightly faster time. Turner qualified earlier, so, as at Indianapolis, he eventually led the 75-car field toward the green flag.

Drivers came from around the country to compete. Herschel McGriff, who didn't retire until 2002, drove his 1950 Oldsmobile from Portland, Oregon to Darlington, painted the number 52 on its roof and doors, and competed with Oregon license plates still in place. After the race, he drove the car back to Oregon.

The drivers were lined up three abreast at the starting line, again matching the Indianapolis model. Brasington and France did not disguise what race they were challenging for supremacy.

Fans knew it and welcomed the new event. Brasington was startled to find overflow crowds filling the few motels long before the green flag waved. He opened up the infield so that 6,000 spectators would have a place to sleep. Naturally, they started another NASCAR tradition — the all-night, infield party.

"Partying is as much a part of the Darlington experience as watching cars and suffering in the stifling heat. In the old days, if you went in the infield here on Sunday night," said Barney Hall, a MRN announcer who has called NASCAR races on radio for more than 44 years, "you'd better be prepared to get into a fistfight or a card game or a drinking contest." [4]

France and Brasington were hoping for 10,000 fans for the inaugural Southern 500. They were astounded when 25,000 showed up, each paying $5.

"We were scared we'd miss the race," owner Junie Dunlavey told *Daily Press* columnist Al Pearce in 2002. "We didn't want to be in traffic, so we left Florence (South Carolina) at midnight and went to the track. We slept on the ground, but at least we were there. I mean, there were people everywhere. When the motels and rooming houses filled up, the track started letting people in the infield. They didn't have anywhere else to stay." [5]

Drivers were scared, but eager to compete.

"Oh, it was a big, big deal," Dunlavey continued. "People started talking about it early in the season, when it was five or six months away. Everybody wanted to be there because it was something special. We'd run modifieds at Langhorne, Pa. (a 1-mile dirt track), but Darlington looked much bigger. I mean, it was this big ol' bowl full of asphalt."

Like France, Dunlavey didn't know if his car could endure the pace or the distance. "My first thought was, 'Hey, ain't no way in the world it'll work,' " he told Pearce. "We knew it would be fun being there, but I don't know if anybody thought stock cars would last that long. The other thing was, it was the first paved track anybody had ever seen, and it was banked to boot. We didn't know about tires or springs or shocks or stuff like that..." [6]

To limit problems during the race, most of the drivers stayed on the bottom of track and avoided the banking completely. Still, there were bouts of nervousness. One driver reportedly darted into the pits, upset because his cigarette lighter wasn't working.

France got involved in more than promoting. He co-owned a 1950 Plymouth Deluxe two-door sedan which was driven by Californian Johnny Mantz in the race. The car, like much of early NASCAR history, is shrouded in a thick fog of misinformation.

Depending on the source, Mantz was hanging around NASCAR's temporary headquarters in a Darlington hotel looking for a ride when France gave him the seat. Or, Mantz had bought the car in California, drove it cross country to the race, then drove it home.

Or, as historian Branham told Bob Christ in 2000, "Mantz bought a Plymouth off a showroom floor in Florence." In this version, Mantz removed all the lights, tied the doors shut with leather straps and joined the field. Then, again, France supposedly bought the car in Darlington to run errands and decided belatedly to enter the Southern 500 after the Plymouth had piled up miles running errands. Or, maybe France sent Mantz to buy the car to handle the small trips around town. One account said the car, which had a six-cylinder engine as opposed to the V-8 engines that powered the other cars, was co-owned by France, polesitter Turner, and NASCAR starter and flagman Alvin Hawkins. Mechanic Hubert Westmoreland was also given a share for tuning the car, according to author Mike Hembree in *The Definite Book of America's Sports*.

There was no such confusion about the driver. Mantz, at least, knew how to handle the Plymouth, which was number 98Jr. to match the number on the Indianapolis car Mantz occasional drove for J.C. Agajanian. A part-time Hollywood stunt man, Mantz had competed in the 1948 and 1949 Indianapolis 500 and was later elected into the National Sprint Car Hall of Fame. He piled up a string of victories on West Coast tracks and was hardly a novice in 1950. He was also better prepared to run on asphalt, having competed on that kind of track elsewhere. Reportedly, he put tough truck tires on the Plymouth akin to those used at Indianapolis and resolved to drive slowly, but steadily, around the new track, confident the bigger cars would wear out before his car.

At 11 am, the same time Indianapolis began its race, under a hot South Carolina sun and in front of the overflow crowd, then-Governor Strom Thurmond and his wife, Jean, cut the ribbon and officially christened the Southern 500. Turner led the field down the front stretch. Befitting his late entry, Mantz started 43rd. Ironically, that used to be the last spot in modern NASCAR Sprint Cup Series races.

"It looked like a bunch of New York taxicabs when they threw the flag," said the late Tim Flock, who eventually was banned from NASCAR for union activities. "The track was dusty. Man, you couldn't see a thing going into the first turn after the first or second lap. It was mayhem."

For more than six hours, the cars continued to circle the track. Few went very far without stopping as tires continually blew. Red Byron, a wounded war vet who was the 1949 NASCAR champion, ran through 24 tires. Turner destroyed 27. The track surface, a mixture of asphalt, sand and crushed sea shells, simply ate through the rubber. Some teams took to searching through the parking lot for replacements. Dunlavey was actually stopped mid-heist by an irate fan, who acquiesced once he learned why the tires were being removed.

Dunleavy fielded a 1949 Oldsmobile for Bob Apperson and relief driver Runt Harris. The team rolled off 49th and finished 61st, running out of tires after 241 of 400 laps. "I had a good, short-track set of racing slicks set aside for late in the race," Dun-leavy said, "but we used it early because we used tires so fast. There were a lot of blown tires and mechanical breakdowns that day." [7]

"I never changed so many tires in my life," said long-time driver/owner, Bud Moore, who won 63 races in his career. "And, we didn't have power tools back then. I know one thing, it was hot, and we were going to the infield and jacking people's cars up to get their tires." [8]

"It was strictly chaos, like it is now," said Richard Petty, who would eventually accumulate more wins than any other driver in NASCAR history, including the 1967 Southern 500.

Ignoring the debris, Mantz kept going. He ended up with the trophy, averaging 76.260 mph, a record for the time although barely above the speed limit on interstates today. He made fewer stops and needed fewer tire changes than anyone. As a result, he finished nine laps ahead of Glenn "Fireball" Roberts, who came home second. For the win, Mantz pocketed $10,510 and, suppos-edly, drove the car back to California after a thorough post-race inspection. No one could believe the little car had outrun its more-powerful competitors, but the car passed scrutiny.

Mantz actually won more money in that one race than Bill Rexford made for winning the 1950 series championship ($6,175).

A car purported to be the winning Plymouth sits in the Dar-lington Hall of Fame at the track, but NASCAR Hall of Fame archivist Buz McKim said that it must be a replica. He said the real Plymouth was driven in several more races before being demolished in a 1951 crash.

After the first Southern 500 ended, everyone packed up to head for Langhorne, Pennsylvania and the next race two weeks later.

"I don't think anyone there had any idea what that day mean for stock car racing," Dunlavey said.

France did. For the first time, he had demonstrated that a stock car could compete for 500 miles, pitting his roughneck sport squarely against the more stylish Indianapolis versions. In addition, he showed that a stock car race could draw a crowd, even to distant and humble Darlington.

This one race literally saved the sport from oblivion. Promoters began to erect larger tracks. Brasington, who eventually lost control of Darlington Raceway, quickly build North Carolina Speedway in Rockingham, another tiny town, which was located about an hour north of Darlington. Dirt tracks, with their enveloping dust and small size, slowly began to fade away.

Darlington began the era when the "paved speedway was born. It quickly became a staple on the Grand National circuit, next to the traditional bullring dirt tracks of state and county fairgrounds. Dirt ovals were still the mainstay, but by the end of the decade it was clear that pavement racing was becoming more and more popular with the fans." [9]

"We loved the dirt tracks," said Richard Petty, who stood in the infield and watched his father, Lee, compete in the first Southern 500. "They were an equalizer. There, the driver made the difference. When I first started running dirt tracks, Joe Weatherly and Curtis Turner won all the races. They were good on dirt. I mean, they'd run sideways down the straightaway. But, the bigger the track and the faster you run, the more you depend on the car."

Fans came, allowing NASCAR to pocket more money, pay larger purses and slowly oust other racing organizations. By the time the AAA pulled out of sanctioning in the 1950s, following the deaths of drivers and/or spectators at Indianapolis and Le Mans, France, NASCAR was in position to assume that role for stock cars.

Darlington held the key to the sport's future. For the first time, stock car racing declared itself equal to Indianapolis. Stock car racing began to shed its rough-hewn image for the patina of gentility and sportsmanship.

Said announcer Hall, looking back across more than four decades of stock car racing success and growth, "It all started at Darlington."

CHAPTER 4: 1969
THE STRIKE

Despite the success of the Southern 500, NASCAR remained barely a blip on the national scene. By 1969, the sanctioning body was now the largest in stock car racing, but its drivers were not taking home much money. Top baseball players were making $1 million a year while Bobby Isaac, who won 17 races that year, banked only $92,074 while competing in a longer, infinitely more dangerous season. Only four drivers in 1969 topped the $100,000 mark, led by champion David Pearson who earned $229,760. And, they weren't happy about it.

Driver Bobby Allison, another star, pointed out that the NASCAR insurance, for example, was laughable, even if it was Frances' key inducement for drivers. If driver gets killed, Allison complained, "His wife gets $15,000, and that's it."

Weeks before the opening of Alabama International Motor Speedway in Talladega Alabama, the drivers had met quietly at Michigan Speedway to discuss a possible union. They were encouraged by Larry LoPatin, a real estate developer who built the Michigan track, among others. Backed by Ford Motor Co., LoPatin wanted to wrest control of NASCAR from France, or, if necessary, start a separate sanctioning body. Almost all of the leading drivers, including Petty, Allison and his brother, Donnie,

David Pearson, LeeRoy Yarbrough and Cale Yarborough joined
the new union. They called themselves the Professional Drivers
Association (PDA) and geared up for the inevitable confrontation
with Bill France.

What happened during those few days in mid-September
forever changed motor sports. More importantly, it guaranteed
that stock car racing would survive. Had the PDA endured, racing
would have faced the kinds of situation that shut down professional
basketball and football, led to the elimination of the 1994 World
Series in baseball and the 2004-2005 National Hockey League
season.

"The problems the other sports have had certainly have benefited us," said Dale Jarrett, the son of a champion racer and a
long-time NASCAR competitor. "There are people I know that
were never fans of stock car racing who have said they always
were football, baseball or basketball fans, but something always
seems to happen where their team's not playing. But, they know
we're going to be there racing."

France's adamant approach to a union probably preserved
stock car racing, which was still spinning its wheels. It had no
television contract; little national recognition. A strike probably
would have been the death knell, especially for NASCAR, which
still relied on weekend receipts simply to keep going.

This was not the first time that drivers had tried to organize,
although the initial attempt was more of a desperate move by a
competitor better known for his late-night escapades than any
serious union activities.

Curtis Turner, a Virginia lumberman who drank and cavorted
his way through several fortunes, decided in 1959 to build a
speedway in Charlotte, North Carolina. He said later the move
was essentially a whim. If so, it was an expensive one.

"Pops," a nicknamed picked up because of Turner's malicious

habit of "popping" a lead car's rear bumper to force it aside, had $2 million in loans when he ordered bulldozers onto the site. Unfortunately for Turner, the dirt turned out to be located on top of a wall of granite, which ran under the end of the proposed speedway and about half the infield. [1]

By the time dynamite cleared the impediment, Turner had sunk $500,000 into what was becoming a deep pit. Lacking the funds now to pay for the rest of the work, he scrounged up every dime he could. Still, in June 1960, part of the track was still unpaved even though the announced race was a few days away. To compound matters, an unpaid contractor vowed to stick his heavy equipment on the track and block any race cars unless Turner came up with the promised dough. Instead, the enterprising driver allegedly showed up brandishing a revolver and got the track completed. The race went on as scheduled.

Still, Turner was so far in debt that even three races a year at the track, currently called Lowe's Motor Speedway, wasn't enough. He needed some help and found a willing benefactor. His name was James Hoffa, the head of the Teamsters Union who was destined to disappear and become the central character in one of this country's enduring mysteries. Hoffa wanted to organize drivers into a Federation of Professional Athletes. Turner agreed to help in exchange for the necessary cash. He started talking up the union. That drew some interest until France heard about it.

According to a column in the *Charlotte Observer*, "France laid it on the line to the drivers: 'Before I have a union stuffed down my throat I will plow up the track in Daytona and, after the next race, no known union member can compete in a NASCAR race.'" [2]

In another account, he reportedly said: "No known Teamster member can compete in a NASCAR race, and I'll use a pistol to enforce it." [3]

His comments were ironic: France had joined with a union to co-sponsor his early beach races in Daytona. However, he didn't join a union, and he was not about to let his drivers enroll either.

To complete dismantling any union idea, France issued a lifetime suspension to Turner, a friend and former co-driver in a lengthy Mexican race, along with the only driver who continued to support Turner, Tim Flock. Turner sued, citing the right-to-work laws, but lost the case. He also lost the Speedway to creditors.

Four years later, France said that Turner and Flock "had paid the penalty" and reinstated them. Actually, both were name drivers. Promoters pressured France because they felt the duo would help sell more tickets. Economics, then and now, ruled race-related decisions. Turner did return and raced for several years before being killed in a plane crash. Flock stayed retired.

The suspensions didn't hurt France's opinion of Turner. In 1972, two years after Turner died, France called him "the greatest race car driver I have ever seen." Flock didn't forget him either. He characterized Turner as "the greatest driver who ever ran in NASCAR."

In 1969, the drivers who formed PDA carried far more weight with fans than either Turner or Flock, but France would not back down then either.

The situation came to a boil in September 1969 when the new track, a sister to Daytona International Speedway, was ready to host its first race. Now named Talladega Superspeedway, the place was downright scary, even to hardened drivers who regularly competed on high-speed, paved tracks.

Located on a former soybean farm next to a couple of abandoned airport runways, the track remains the biggest and fastest motor sports facility in the world. Banked at 33 degrees, the facility extends 2.66 miles around and helps cars generate speeds well in excess of 200 mph down the mammoth 4,000-foot backstretch. Before restrictor plates were required to slow down the cars, Bill Elliott set the stock car qualifying record by averaging 212.809 mph there in 1987. In another race, every driver qualified at more than 200 mph.

The high speed was intentional. France had decided to build the track on a scale that would dwarf Daytona and Indianapolis. He hired a local engineer, Bill Moss, to do the work.

Moss was working on U.S. 20 through Talladega when the county commission brought him and France together. "He wanted to build the biggest and fastest track," recalled Moss, a civil engineering graduate from the University of Alabama who went on to build Las Vegas Motor Speedway and the Kentucky Speedway, among others. Talladega definitely is huge: the oval cost about $9.5 million to construct across nearly 2,000 acres.

France's real target continued to be Indianapolis, the *bete noir* of his life. In 1954, the AAA had ousted France from The Brickyard during time trials. The sanctioning body made it clear that it did not consider stock cars equal to the Indy cars.

"We have a longstanding disagreement with NASCAR on what constitutes good racing," an AAA official was quoted in an Associated Press report of the incident.

In retaliation, France built Daytona International Speedway in 1959 and swore he would get drivers to post higher speeds than at Indianapolis. Marvin Panch won the 1961 Daytona 500, averaging a higher speed for the entire race than the pole speed for the Indianapolis 500 that year. Talladega was simply France's latest move to overshadow what was still the capital of American motor sports. If Talladega blocked some of Daytona's glow, France didn't care as long as Indianapolis was also in the dark.

He succeeded. The 33-degree banked turns are the second highest on the NASCAR circuit — Bristol Motor Speedway has

36-degree turns — and allowed stock cars to break the 200-mph barrier in the early 1970s when cars at Indianapolis were topping out at about 170 mph.

"Bill France Sr. was a visionary, and he knew where NASCAR was going," Moss said. "He told me he wanted the infrastructure in place to seat 200,000 people. I think it's one of our greatest accomplishments. It's an engineering marvel that I don't think anything in the state can touch."[4]

Drivers in 1969 were definitely overawed. Moreover, they quickly discovered that the racing tires supplies by manufacturers could not stand up to the track. Goodyear and Firestone kept testing their tires during the week leading up to the race. Each day, their engineers promised better results. Each day, test tires blew up at high speed. Finally, Firestone packed up its equipment and walked away. Goodyear was going to exit, too, but France convinced the company representatives to stay. Today, Goodyear remains the only official supplier of tires to all three NASCAR national touring series. Then, however, the company still hadn't figured out the right compound for tires by Friday, a day before the first race.

As a result, in one of its first official decisions, members of the PDA voted to boycott the race. "Four laps would tear the tires off the car at speed," Petty said.

PDA members did not tell France immediately of their boycott plans. Instead, Petty and Donnie Allison tried to talk to him.

"There was a bunch of controversy," Petty said. "We went back and forth with France. We talked in front of people, behind the doors, everywhere. He was bound and determined that he was going to run the race, no matter what. The drivers were bound and determined they weren't going to run. France was looking at it from his standpoint with NASCAR and his involvement with the race track. We were looking at it as our survival."

France refused to back down. He had no choice. Talladega was designed to bring in money when Daytona was idle. He couldn't afford to cancel the race. He responded to demands with sarcasm: "Some of these fellows have gotten to be big heroes and they have apparently forgotten how they got there," he told reporters. "I can't see why LeeRoy Yarbrough, for instance, would want such a group. He's won $150,000 this year alone. That's not too bad."

France told the complaining drivers that, if they thought the tires wouldn't last, to slow down.

"He said run just fast enough to keep the tires from coming apart," Petty said. "Well, that doesn't work with drivers. They're going to run as cotton-picking hard as they can all the time because that's their job."

The union went public with its concerns. "We really weren't organized," Petty said. "Then we got to Talladega, and the group said let's talk to them, say we want to run the race. We just don't want to run it under these circumstances."

Petty said he suggested to France, "Just do it like a rainout. We're not calling off the race. The race will run, just next week or whatever. Give the manufacturers a chance to build us a good tire."

On Saturday morning, Petty gave no doubt of his decision. He loaded up his trailer and waited for France to concede. He did not know that France had actually borrowed a Ford for a private test. Then nearly 60, the stubborn czar of stock car racing climbed into the car and turned laps safely at 176 mph. He emerged from the car convinced the drivers could compete if they went a little slower. "If a 60-year-old man can drive 176," he said defiantly, "surely our top drivers can do it safely at 20 miles over that."

In a later essay that appeared in the April 1970 issue of *Motor Trend*, France said that he could not stop the race. People had purchased tickets, he explained, and he didn't want to disappoint them. He also claimed not to known about the boycott until it was too late to respond. That's probably a rewrite of history. PDA had signaled concern about the track for weeks, and talk of a boycott circulated in the media prior to the race. France probably lacked the cash to provide refunds.

While Petty sat in his trailer, France made a public announcement: "All brave race drivers are invited to participate," he said.

That was enough for Petty. He started his engine. So did a row of trailers awaiting his signal. One by one, lights on, horns blaring, they pulled out of the parking area and headed down the road. France never blinked.

"He kind of panicked. We kind of panicked," Petty insisted. [5]

The first NASCAR race that weekend ran on Saturday and featured drivers not in the top tier, the Grand National Division. Everyone naturally watched to see what would happen. Nothing unusual did. Ken Rush won the 'BAMA 400 Grand Touring race. He was the 1957 Grand National Rookie of the Year who had been relegated to the second level of NASCAR.

The real question was whether fans, expecting the top drivers, would come to the big race on Sunday. To encourage them, France ingeniously shifted the credit by announcing that the directors of the Speedway had voted to give one free ticket for an upcoming race at this track or in Daytona to everyone who came to this one. A full house took advantage of the offer.

Few regular drivers joined a 36-car field which included Bobby Isaac, who would win the 1970 NASCAR Grand National Division title, and Tiny Lund, who was driving Bill France's entry. As an indication how many of the best-known drivers participated, only seven were awarded points in the Grand National Series standings, the forerunner of the Winston Cup and then Sprint Cup circuit. That name will change again as Sprint decided not to renew its sponsorship. Sprint has been replaced by Monster Energy, starting with the 2017 season.

Isaac was second in the standing and wouldn't have been expected to buck the PDA, but the moody North Carolina native had few friends among the drivers. He wasn't invited to join the PDA, so felt no compunction to side with boycotting union members.

"It kind of hurt my feelings," Isaac explained a couple of years later in an interview for *Circle Track and Highway* magazine. "My car owner asked me not to make any quick decisions. I don't belong to the PDA, but I don't condemn anybody for being a member." [6]

He definitely didn't mind speed. A year later, in 1970, Isaac would set the speed record for a closed course, by tearing around Talladega at 201.104 mph. He then set 28 world class records on the Bonneville (Utah) Salt Flats in his Dodge. In 1973, midway during a race at Talladega, he simply stopped his car and said he had decided to quit. Later, he told Buddy Baker that voices told him to stop. After an abortive comeback begun two years later, Isaac died of a heart attack in 1977 while competing in a short-track race at Hickory, North Carolina. Ironically, Isaac had made his debut years before at that track.

Richard Brickhouse was another Grand National regular who chose to compete. He had joined the PDA, but had the announcer broadcast his resignation from the union. Then, he climbed into the car vacated by the striking Charlie Glotzbach.

"At that point in my career, I felt obligated to honor my contract. I had signed a contract to race in the Alabama 500 and that's what I did," Brickhouse said. "I had a good relationship with Bill France and didn't want to jeopardize it."

Glotzbach had won the pole, while Brickhouse started the race in ninth place.

Everyone drove carefully. There were seven cautions, but only because NASCAR wanted drivers into the pits to change tires. Late in the race, Brickhouse picked up the pace and pulled away for an easy win.

France met him in Victory Lane with the trophy. Decades later, Brickhouse still remembered shaking hands with the leathery NASCAR chairman. "I think that's the only time he ever presented a trophy to the driver in Victory Lane," Brickhouse said proudly.

Naturally, he, Isaac and the handful of non-striking colleagues were targets of verbal abuse. Reportedly, there were also mishaps on the track triggered by angry union drivers. Still, Isaac won the race at Columbia, South Carolina that was held the week after Talladega. The union had no future anyway. Fans made that clear by supporting the series despite the boycott. In pre-race introductions prior to the next race, Isaac received the loudest ovation.

There would be no more unions, no threats of boycotts, no dent in the dictatorial control Bill France — and his successors — would have over NASCAR. The sport had survived this threat. Still, France did not have a lot of money. Teams that relied on support from automobile manufacturers suddenly faced a growing deficit. Chevrolet had pulled out of NASCAR in the mid-1960s; Ford and Dodge were threatening to follow suit.

France and stock car racing had somehow endured for 22 tumultuous years. Only a miracle would help the sport last a few years more.

CHAPTER 5: 1971
THE ARRIVAL OF R.J. REYNOLDS TOBACCO CO.

May 16, 1971, on a Sunday afternoon in Alabama, drivers in NASCAR's top series lined up for the start of another race at Alabama International Motor Speedway. The stands were full; the traditional, deep-throated sounds of race engines filled the air. None of that was unusual. Donnie Allison had won the pole and would win the race. That was not strange either. Allison would capture 10 races before a severe 1981 accident abbreviated his career and was then part of what was known as the "Alabama Gang" of competitors who enjoyed great success through the 1980s.

What was different was the name of the race. It was called the Winston 500, the first of only four of the 48 point races that year to bear the name of a sponsor. Winston gave its name to two of those four races, marking the beginning of the most lucrative and successful business partner in sports history. In 1970, the R.J. Reynolds Tobacco Co. decided to link up with stock car racing. That decision insured that the sport would endure. No other sport is more dependent on sponsor support; no other sport owes its survival to a single company.

The connection between them began with an old racer looking for some cash to keep his team on the track.

In 1973, one-time moonshine runner Junior Johnson was inducted in the National Motorsports Press Association's Hall of Fame at Darlington Raceway. In 1990, he was inducted into the International Motorsports Hall of Fame in Talladega.

In 1970, however, he was only a man with an idea at a time when corporate support for stock car racing was drying up. Johnson, by then a car owner, didn't know where he'd get the cash to compete for another season in NASCAR's premier series, the Grand National Division after his sponsor — an auto-parts dealer from Detroit — had died in a plane crash.

His attention was caught by news reports regarding cigarette manufacturers, who faced major changes in their marketing plans. In 1969, the tobacco industry "offered to discontinue all advertising on radio and television," according to an Internet report. Congress "accepted that offer" in 1970, and tobacco advertisements were banned from airwaves starting on January 2, 1971.

Johnson wondered why some of the unused money couldn't be routed into worthy teams like his that were now famished for support.

"As quick as I could get a meeting with R.J. Reynolds, that's what I wanted," Johnson told a NASCAR *Winston Scene* columnist, in July 2003. He made the trip from his home in Wilkes County to Winston-Salem and asked RJR to sponsor his race car for a year at a cost of about $100,000.

According to the story, the meeting took place in early 1971. Actually, the meeting happened in early 1970, former NASCAR vice president Jim Foster said. Foster's timetable is more plausible. Correspondence between Bill France and RJR's Arthur Weber, dated Dec. 4, 1970, refers to an earlier agreement dated November 30, 1970. Johnson's supposed 1971 meeting would have been after the pact was reached.

"I came in there looking for sponsorship money," Johnson

told R.A. "Bob" Rechholtz, vice president of marketing and Art Weber, manager of marketing services, in a corporate account published in 1985. "They said they wanted something bigger — a bigger deal."

According to published accounts, Johnson actually asked for $500,000 — even though T. Wayne Robertson, who later led RJR sports marketing program, said in a 1997 interview that a car in 1970 could be sponsored for as little as $25,000.

Johnson's request for $500,000 drew only a blank stare. Johnson's friend, RJR salesman W. Ralph Seagraves replied, "Look, we just got booted off television. We were thinking along the lines of $800 million or $900 million."

Johnson recalled being stunned. "That's some ungodly figure you're willing to spend," he said and then arranged for RJR officials to meet with Bill France. "They needed to do more than sponsor a race car, mine or any others," Johnson said.

He flew to Daytona Beach with Seagraves, who worked in the Washington, D.C. area, to meet with France. However, they weren't carrying startling news to NASCAR headquarters in Daytona Beach. Although Johnson didn't know it, France has already started discussions with Rechholtz and Weber. The men came prepared to make a deal. They had already begun the search for alternative advertising venues now that American media was closing to tobacco products and had visited a variety of sporting events in Europe, including racing, soccer and horseracing.

Tony Zaffuto, then a vice president of marketing at RJR, recalls that officials at the company felt the demographics of cigarette smokers and race fans matched up perfectly. Now retired after teaching marketing courses for many years at Daytona State College (Florida), Zaffuto said RJR had purchased a liquor company earlier that year. At the time, Zaffuto facetiously suggested that RJR consider working out something with prostitution so that it could market all the "socially accepted vices." He said his bosses didn't see the humor in that proposal.

France wanted RJR to sponsor the entire Grand National Division series. He flew back to RJR headquarters in Winston-Salem, North Carolina with that proposal. RJR wasn't prepared to go that far. Weber "explained that RJR would be more inclined to sponsor a major race," according to the company account.

They decided to meet again in March 1970 to hammer out the details.

At that point, France played his last trump card. He invited Weber and his wife to the 1970 Daytona 500 in February.

"I had never seen a race on a superspeedway," said Weber, whose European travels had taken him only to road courses. "My eyes were opened. I saw all kinds of advertising opportunities."

By the time, NASCAR and RJR officials met in Winston-Salem in March, everyone was in agreement on sponsorship.

No one was breaking new ground. Rival tobacco companies were already involved with racing. *Motorsport*, an English publication, reported that by 1971, Liggett & Myers already supported the Sports Car Club of America (SCCA) Continental Series, while Marlboro, a Philip Morris brand, was the sponsor of the United States Auto Club (USAC) Championship Trail. Like RJR, they needed to find some place to advertise.

At the March meeting, France was joined by his son, Bill Jr., then-vice president of NASCAR and general manager of the International Speedway Corporation, and by Foster, then-NASCAR public relations director. Representing RJR was Rechholtz, Weber and Bob O'Dear, Winston's product manager.

RJR Chairman of the Board, Bob Smith, came by and was immediately given a France sales pitch. "He tried to convince me that NASCAR could put Winston on the map," Smith recalled.

Actually, at the time, Smith noted with a chuckle, Winston

had long been the No. 1 selling cigarette in the world.

Smith may have laughed, but the humor was hollow. Winston actually no longer held the lofty ranking in sales, but had fallen behind Marlboro and its cowboy image. Prior to the government crackdown on televised cigarette advertising, RJR had ridden Winston and its familiar, ungrammatical jingle, "Winston tastes good like a cigarette should," to the top spot. However, without audio, the song seemed flat and almost effeminate. Marlboro charged into the lead. RJR Reynolds needed something to recast Winston with a masculine style. What could have been better than stock car racing with its gruff exterior and reputation for lusty, manly collisions on and off the track?

The two sides quickly got down to work. RJR had no trouble fulfilling its own goal by agreeing to sponsor the 1971 spring race in Talladega already touted as the fastest track in the world. At the same time, NASCAR got what it wanted — a promise by RJR representatives to consider sponsoring the entire series.

The agreement proposed in the November 30, 1970 letter sent by Rechholtz and signed later by France on behalf of NASCAR offered as its first point to rename the "annual contest" to "Winston Cup." Rechholtz said the company "will adopt a symbol to be owned by us and used in publicizing the Contest."

As part of the agreement, all drivers were obligated to wear the emblem on the "chest of their uniforms" and place it "on the racing cars driven by them in a uniform location on both sides of the quarter panel of the vehicle."

The company also agreed to set up a $50,000 fund to reward drivers twice during the year and again at the end of the season. The top seven drivers would split $25,000 after 33 percent and then 66 percent of the races had been run, followed by $25,000 to be divided among the top seven drivers after the final race.

That changed a month later, when RJR unilaterally doubled its ante.

"We have elected to increase the amount of the 'Winston Cup' prize fund," Weber wrote. "We feel that this increase will provide Grand National drivers a more significant incentive than the $50,000 level we had originally planned."

The new level was higher than all but five drivers earned in all of 1970. Despite competing in 47 of the 48 races scheduled that year, champion Bobby Isaac that year topped the money list by winning $199,000, followed by Richard Petty ($151,124), Bobby Allison ($149,705), Pete Hamilton ($131,406) and Cale Yarborough ($115,875). No one else reached the $100,000 plateau.

To make the investment pay off, RJR purchased billboards around each track to promote races. The company bought newspaper ads and created promotions with local retail chains in each market.

To oversee the effort, Smith named Seagraves as director of RJR's new Special Events Department, which had been founded in December 1970 to handle the racing promotion. Seagraves was almost as tall as France and fit right into the stock car crowd. Although forced to wear a suit for his job, he occasionally slid under a car with a wrench in his hand.

He was later succeeded by T. Wayne Robertson, whose first job with RJR had been to take a cheesy-looking show car to various events, mainly held at shopping centers across the South. The car had no body and carried a three-sided sign on it that told spectators who the point leaders were in the Grand National circuit and where the next race would be.

The department was eventually renamed as Sports Marketing Enterprises and, at one time, became separated from RJR. Later, it was integrated back into the company. The big tobacco company also branched out into drag racing, motorcycle racing, golf and additional sports. Consumer groups raised complaints that RJR was circumventing the ban on advertising, but failed to have an impact.

A North Carolina native, Seagraves was looking to help the company to "get involved with sports that were compatible with our marketing needs. The key has been that the events need us, and we need them. Together, we make big happenings."

They exceeded that plan. R.J. Reynolds' modest excursion into sports marketing revolutionized the field and heralded the beginning of what NASCAR calls the "Modern Era."

The impact of on NASCAR was immediate and affected virtually every aspect of the stock car racing world.

Race Lengths

In 1970, 19 of the 48 NASCAR Grand National Division races were less than 250 miles in length. The July 7 event that year, the Albany-Saratoga 250 at Albany-Saratoga Speedway in Malta, New York, was the shortest — 90.5 miles on a .362-mile paved track.

RJR insisted that races must be a minimum of 250 miles in order to have enough time for marketing efforts. The schedule was set for 1971, so the new length requirement went into effect a year later. In 1971, 16 of the 48 races were less than 250 miles long. In 1972, none were. That remains true today.

Race Tracks

By requiring a minimum length, RJR limited race venues. Between 1971 and 1972, 16 tracks vanished from the schedule. That was probably a good thing. Few promoters were making money. Most tracks, at best, were shabby and uninviting. Seagraves' first task was supplying red and white paint, Winston's colors, to spruce up the tracks.

In 1971, 18 tracks on the schedule hosted at least two races. Daytona Beach had four. After RJR conditions went into effect, all but two tracks — Ontario (California) Motor Speedway and the New Jersey State Fairgrounds in Trenton — hosted two races. Ontario, a 2.5-mile paved track, was new to the schedule in 1971. Trenton, a 1-mile paved track that had been off and on the schedule since 1958, never hosted another premier NASCAR race after 1972.

The length requirement also spurred construction of new tracks to accommodate NASCAR races. Tracks in the early years were often dirt and short, typically about .5-miles around. After RJR arrived, tracks remained small. Paved, high-speed tracks were limited to Atlanta, Charlotte, Darlington and Daytona Beach until 1969 when Alabama International Motor Superspeedway in Alabama was added.

Gradually, that track dimensions increased. Of the 22 tracks used in the 2004 NASCAR Sprint Cup Series, eight (more than 33 percent) were built after 1971. All of the newer tracks are at least 1.5-miles around. In 2015, the top NASCAR series tours 23 tracks. Only two are road course. Most are 1.5 miles. Small tracks are now limited to Bristol, Martinsville and Richmond, all of which date from the 1940s and are traditional venues.

The newer tracks are all paved. The image of swirling dirt, which obscured cars, fans and signs, didn't appeal to the new sponsor. NASCAR drivers competed on dirt for the last time on Sept. 30, 1970, a 100-mile race held on the State Fairgrounds in Raleigh, N.C. Richard Petty posted an average speed of 68.376 mph and took home $1,000 along with the checkered flag.

RJR's impact on the tracks was limited in only one area: Tracks then and now are still scattered from Florida to Maine and as far west as California. Races over the years have been held in at least 34 different states as well as in two cities in Canada.

Stability

In 1970, five of the NASCAR tracks were in bankruptcy, Seagraves reported.

"When we came into the sport in 1971," Robertson told *Racer Magazine* in 1997, "Riverside (California) was ready to close. Atlanta was close to closing. Rockingham (North Carolina) was close to closing. Events were dwindling down, and manufacturers were pulling out."

"For us to be successful," Seagraves continued in a separate interview, "we had to change that."

There was only one solution. "For the first six years of the agreement," Seagraves said, "we had one primary objective in mind: put people in the stands."

The company did more than buy ads. "We assisted in such things as building grandstands, concession, stands, restrooms, sponsor suites, press boxes, scoreboards, expanded garages, bridges, entrance signs and flag stands," Seagraves reported. "We wanted to be associated with a successful enterprise for the long term."

The massive effort paid off. In 1949, NASCAR's first year, maybe 120,000 people showed up to watch the races. Attendance in 1971 was estimated at 900,000. By 1975, about 2 million fans came to NASCAR races. Today, the total is close to 10 million, with millions more watching on television. NASCAR estimates it has 75 million fans — about 37 percent of all Americans.

Attendance has fallen recently as have TV ratings. Nevertheless, millions annually attend motorsports' events around the world.

Race Schedule

NASCAR races were held wherever promoters could be found to set up a track and draw customers. As a result, seasons were very uneven. In 1949, Red Byron became the first NASCAR Strictly Stock champion after winning two of the six races he entered. A year later, Bill Rexford made 17 starts to edge Fireball Roberts for the title. As a side note: Roberts lost by blowing his engine in a futile effort to win the season finale — the paycheck for winning the race was higher than for taking home the championship. In 1951, Herb Thomas finished atop the standings after 34 races. By 1956, the season consisted of 48 races. The number hit 50 in 1958, peaking at 62 in 1964.

R.J. Reynolds insisted on uniformity. The company wanted the stars on the track. Previously, only a handful of drivers ever raced for the championship. It was too expensive for every team to compete in that many races.

In 1971, NASCAR scheduled 48 Grand National races. In 1972, the number was chopped to 31. The two qualifying races for the Daytona 500 were dropped to non-point status and not included on the official schedule. In 1971, no drivers competed in all 48 scheduled races. In 1972, the top six drivers in the point standings competed in all the races.

Before 1971, retired driver Bobby Allison told writer Ben White in 2003, "It was really a tough deal because we ran some Wednesday nights and Thursday nights and Friday nights and Saturday nights and Sundays. Most races paid $1,000 to win and were 100 milers. One night, you might run dirt; and the next night, you would run pavement. It was real carnival, sporadic deal. Some days were a really big deal; and some days, it was small enough that you would know everybody in the area."

That changed when RJR arrived, he said.

"R.J. Reynolds Tobacco Company brought class to stock car racing. They brought importance, and they helped move it into being a major league sport. It was sandlot baseball, and R.J.R. took it to around 30 major events a year instead of 50 or 55 that included some major events and lots of minor events," Allison said.

Drivers

Sponsorship had a calming effect on the sport and widened its appeal.

For decades, drivers were the same roughnecks who battled on and off the track, waged feuds, threw punches and helped produce the aura of spontaneity and excitement surrounding the sport.

Clifton "Coo-Coo" Marlin had to talk his way out of jail simply to compete in the 1972 Firecracker 400 after he, his wife, Eula Faye, and fellow drivers Elmo Langley and Dub Simpson got too near a brawl at a Daytona Beach nightspot. One of the two men fighting accidentally struck Marlin's wife. The Tennessean promptly jumped into the fray along with his colleagues.

"We were ahead when the police finally came by," Marlin reported proudly.

Melees took place on and off the track. That was not the image R.J. Reynolds or any sponsor wanted.

RJR took immediate control by requiring all participating drivers sign an agreement that allowed the company "to use his name, his photos and photos of his racing vehicles in any and all advertising and promotional material issued in connection with the contest ..."

Mug shots were obviously not an option.

Good behavior not only ensured that a driver received publicity, but, in time, helped guarantee sponsorship. In 2002, when Tony Stewart was accused of striking a photographer and a fan in separate incidents, he was not reprimanded by NASCAR. Instead, his sponsor, Home Depot, warned him that further incidents could jeopardize his ride. Stewart became (mostly) a model citizen.

As a result, NASCAR has not been plagued by the kind of sordid incidents that have damaged other sports. NBA players and fans exchanged punches in a 2004 slugfest, but only cars have gone into the stands during stock car races. Actually, drivers are known as the most accessible of major sports figures, often accosted in the garages prior to a race by fans seeking autographs. Drivers still have piques of temper, but incidents have been very limited and draw attention because of their rarity.

Drivers

Born in the Deep South, racing drew working-class men, whom fans — almost all of whom lived in that region — could understand and bond with. Virtually all the top NASCAR drivers in the early years spoke with a Southern drawl: Richard Petty, Cale Yarborough, David Pearson, Buck and Buddy Baker, Bobby and Donnie Allison, among others. The need for a southern tie was so intense that driver Jack Smith, who was born in Illinois and lived there until he was 6, actually insisted he was from Georgia. His nickname was "Cracker" Jack, emphasizing the southern influence.

Competitors in NASCAR events started driving along dirt roads between small towns in rural areas, took their souped-up sedans to tiny, unpaved bullrings where the dust flew faster than the cars.

From 1956 to 1980, almost every NASCAR champ came from North Carolina, South Carolina and Virginia.

Since 1980, only champions Dale Earnhardt, Bobby Allison, Bill Elliott and Dale Jarrett can claim those traditional southern roots.

The others span the nation: California (Jeff Gordon and Jimmie Johnson), Indiana (Tony Stewart), Kentucky (Darrell Waltrip),

Nevada (Kurt and Kyle Busch), Texas (Bobby and Terry Labonte), Missouri (Rusty Wallace), Wisconsin (Alan Kulwicki, Matt Kenseth).

Drivers have moved to the South to be closer to their teams, but their hometowns are located in at least 17 different states.

RJR national advertising helped expand interest in stock car racing beyond its southern roots. The spread of the sport nationally continues to draw drivers from diverse settings.

As a side effect, today's many successful drivers are younger, too.

At one time, drivers were typically in their 30s before becoming consistent winners. In 2002, drivers who hadn't celebrated their 30th birthday won 18 races. More recently, Trevor Bayne was only 20 when he won the Daytona 500 in 2011. Joey Logano was 24 when he rode off a winner in the 2015 Daytona 500.

Other young drivers now in the top circuit include Chase Elliot (born in 1995), Jeb Burton (born 1992), Alex Bowman (1993), and Austin Dillon (1990).

Graybeards can't help but notice how competitive the young shavers are.

"The younger guys coming into the sport today might be young in years," said Kenny Schrader, who still races occasionally although born in 1955, "but most of them already have a ton of experience driving stock cars. Since the early 1980s, stock car racing has opened up more seats with the NASCAR Truck Series, a stronger ARCA RE/MAX Series and more good NASCAR Xfinity Series rides out there. That gives more young guys a greater chance to get more experience."

"When I came down," added Mark Martin, who was born in 1959, "you were lucky to get in a car that was halfway competitive. The opportunities are much better now than they were in the 1980s."

The younger drivers gathered attention by winning in go-karts and then often moving on to Midgets, Sprint and open-wheel cars. By building local reputations, they attracted sponsors and were able to develop their skills at a very young age.

"I think drivers can come from anywhere in the world and race here in NASCAR," said Jeff Gordon, a California native who retired at the end of 2015 at the age of 44. He started the youth trend by winning his first championship in 1995 when he was 23 years old (see chapter 11). "It doesn't matter where you are from or what kind of upbringing you have. It's important to start young."

That's something no one would have said when racers first came to Daytona International Speedway in 1959. Lee Petty, for example, was 44 when he won the inaugural Daytona 500 that year.

Points

The arrival of RJR also coincided with an effort to work out a comprehensible method of awarding points.

In the early years, title runs were still often nail-biters and a bit strange because of arcane rules for awarding points. Initially, drivers received points based on prize money available at each race. Later, other methods of awarding points would be tried, including length of races, lap leaders and other guideposts.

That led to some bizarre results. In 1961, for example, Rex White raced in one more event than Ned Jarrett, finished with seven wins to Jarrett's one, had more top-five and top-10 finishes and won more money. Jarrett, however, won the championship.

In 1973, Benny Parsons came home with the championship by a mere 67.15 points over Cale Yarborough, although Yarborough had more wins, more top-five finishes and earned more money. To secure his title, Parsons needed help. That year, NASCAR awarded 100 points to the winner of a race and a point for each lap completed. Parsons was up more than 200 points on Yarborough, but 375 points were available to the winner of the finale at North Carolina Speedway.

On lap 13, Parsons was caught up in an accident when Johnny Barnes lost control on turn 1. While Yarborough continued to cruise around "The Rock," Parsons' crew was joined by members of other teams to repair the car and get it back on the track. Parsons managed to limp back to the race, slowly piling up laps and points to clinch his lone title.

Under the next approach, that heroic effort wouldn't have been necessary. Prodded by R.J. Reynolds to develop a coherent system, in 1974, NASCAR turned to Bob Latford, public relations director for Atlanta Motor Speedway. At a race in Talladega that year, former schoolmate Bill France Jr. asked Latford to devise a points system to replace the mishmash of ideas that had developed over the years.

Latford went to Daytona and swapped thoughts with other NASCAR officials. One day after work, they went to the Boot Hill Saloon — famed for its association with motorcyclists and its location across from a cemetery — for some refreshments and sketched out several formulas on cocktail napkins. One idea gave 175 points to a race winner, dropping down to by five, then four and then three by position down through the running order. Drivers who ran up front would receive five bonus points for leading a lap and five for leading the most laps in a race.

Latford compared the system with the previous three years of results and liked the outcome. He then typed up a proposal and submitted it.

It went into effect in 1975. The system increased competition and virtually guaranteed close championship races. Overall, 10 title runs since 1979 have been decided by less than 47 points.

Scoring was not changed until 2004 when extra points were awarded for winning a race and taking the pole position. In addition, under the revised system, drivers compete for 26 races to establish their positions in the standings. Then, the top 12 drivers battle through the final 10 races to determine the champion. The change came after Kenseth easily won the 2003 championship with only one victory, while Ryan Newman languished far behind despite winning a season-high eight races. Ironically, Busch won the 2004 series with three wins, while Jimmie Johnson finished second with eight. Jeff Gordon, in third, had five. However, because of the playoff approach, the championship race was then the closest in NASCAR history.

The scoring system was shaken up again in 2011. The new approach awarded 43 points for a race victory, with three bonus points for winning and one bonus point for leading a lap. A driver could get a 1 point bonus for leading the most laps. In the end, the winner could get 48 points.

The next place finisher got 42 points, with each succeeding position getting 1 less point. That way, everyone was guaranteed at least 1 point with possible extra points for leading a lap and/or leading the most laps.

The whole thing was refined in 2014 with a victory in the first 26 races guaranteeing a driver a spot in the 10-race playoffs, known as the Chase for the NASCAR Sprint Cup. Instead of just the top 12 drivers qualifying, 16 make the field, which is still a smaller percentage of participating teams than in basketball or hockey.

Once the playoff starts, the four lowest scoring drivers are eliminated until, by the last race, only four drivers remain to compete. A driver can guarantee to move on by winning a race during the Chase section.

That can create anomalies. In 2015, the first year this approach was incorporated, Denny Hamlin, Matt Kenseth and Kevin Harvick all won early races, but didn't survive for the final shootout. Joey Logano won three Chase races and didn't make it to the last race at Homestead-Miami. On the other hand, Jeff Gordon won a race and went to the finals. Martin Truex Jr. and Kyle Busch did not win a race in the Chase, but accumulated enough points to join Gordon and Harvick in the final event.

Busch came home first and garnered his first Sprint Cup championship.

Other Series

RJR didn't focus its entire promotional effort on NASCAR's premier series. From the first, NASCAR had included a several subsidiary series, including a Modified Series that ran in the Northeast. Byron, who won the first NASCAR championship, was also the Modified champ that year. At one time, France thought the Modified Series would be NASCAR's ace, only changing his mind after seeing the public response to stock cars.

By 1974, RJR began to underwrite a promotional package for the Late Model Sportsman (now the NASCAR Xfinity Series) and Modified Series. In a letter signed by Roger Bear, Sports Marketing Enterprises group team manager, the company explained its rationale: the program "is designed to attract additional customers to your speedway so that your crowds increase and to make more money. Naturally, when your crowds go, we have an … opportunity to sell cigarettes …"

The proposal called for a promoter to run 10 or more sanctioned weekly races during the season. In return, RJR provided $1,000 cash bonuses to track champions — at a time when a winner of a track championship might not win that much in prize money all season — a "customized Bell helmet" for the big winner and "event promotion support."

There was even a "long range building and paint program" so each track could become a "more appealing and pleasant place to visit. We have developed a color scheme and paint design that is most attractive and is the standard at NASCAR tracks," Bear wrote.

RJR also offered to publicize races at the track and set up phone number "toll free for those outside North Carolina" to keep the company posted on point races and major events.

The Grand National Division, Winston West Series (now K&N Pro West Series) and other series, including ones in Canada, Mexico, Europe and Australia, serve as reminders of this far-sighted program, which has kept racing alive in the rural communities of America and widened interest in the sport. The old bullrings that once hosted NASCAR Cup races now became home to lower-level series featuring local drivers. Drivers could no longer compete in the premier races with cars plucked from used car lots, but weekly drivers could follow that route in a kind of minor league-program akin to baseball. The best drivers, however, could move up the competitive ladder until they reached the top.

K & N Pro West Series drivers, for example, use cars similar to those in the NASCAR Sprint Cup Series and compete twice a year on the same race weekend with NASCAR Sprint Cup drivers. Kevin Harvick, 2001 and 2006 NASCAR Xfinity Series champ and 2001 Sprint Cup Rookie of the Year, caught the attention of car owners after winning at West Series race at California Speedway prior to a NASCAR Sprint Cup event.

Records

R.J. Reynolds modernized NASCAR off the track, too. The company had promised to reward the winner of the series, track champions and the like, but statistics were notoriously inaccurate.

Early NASCAR history is replete with dozens of races where the names of winners were changed because of scoring irregularities. Unlike baseball fans, who regularly keep box scores as cherished mementoes, race records were not seen as valuable. NASCAR didn't have an official archivist until 2003, 55 years after its first race.

Retired *Daytona Beach News-Journal* photographer Chuck Borel recalled raiding trash cans in the mid-1960s to retrieve piles of old race photographs simply discarded by NASCAR officials. "They didn't care," he said. Records were simply sent to Talladega for a race museum there.

Reynolds remedied that by setting up its own department to keep the official records. For years, the company produced the media guides and similar information. NASCAR's history, in fact, has been reconstructed through RJR's records.

As a result of all these improvements and modifications, the R.J. Reynolds Tobacco Co. and NASCAR became wedded in a marriage destined to last 33 years and benefit both sides.

"There is no question that we have to contribute a significant part of our growth ... to Winston," Bill France Jr. said.

The feeling has been mutual. "We, too, have benefited considerably from the sponsorship," said Seagraves, who died in 1998.

Drivers fully appreciate that role.

"When R.J. Reynolds began sponsoring NASCAR Winston Cup races in 1971," driver Richard Petty said, "no one knew it would work out because a major American corporation had never been a series sponsor of a sport like stock car racing. Reynolds and its people associated with NASCAR Winston Cup racing have made a huge impact on the national sports scene. Their well-rounded programs aimed at helping tracks, competitors, the media and fans have also been highly instrumental in the enormous growth of the sport.

"When R.J. Reynolds Tobacco Co. stepped in, it was a God-sent thing for racing."

R.J. Reynolds Tobacco did a lot more than simply add its name to the premier series in stock car racing. The company opened its checkbook and eventually poured millions of dollars into two different bonus pools for competitors.

Matt Kenseth, the 2003 champion, walked away with a $4.25 million bonus check, a $500,000 increase from the 2002 total. Kevin Harvick didn't win the 2015 title, but banked $12.8 million. In contrast, Red Byron received a $1,250 bonus for winning the 1949 championship. That was less than the winner of a single race that year could earn. Byron, for example, won $2,000 for getting the checkers on the Beach-Road Course in Daytona Beach, Florida that year. Bob Flock took home $1,500 for his victory at the North Wilksboro (North Carolina) Speedway.

In 1952, Pure Oil provided contingency money and free gasoline for Daytona's Speedweeks, and Champion Spark Plugs contributed $5,000 to the year-end point fund. Tim Flock won the championship and $20,210 that season.

Scroll ahead a few years. In 1989, Rusty Wallace became the first driver in motorsports to receive a $1 million check for winning the championship. By comparison, no driver had won $1 million in an entire season until 1985.

The pool of money available at the end of the year started at $100,000 in 1971. The total reached $750,000 by 1985. In 2003, the top 25 drivers in the standings shared in a $17 million pot, up $3 million from 2002. That amount has jumped astronomically along with income. In one published account, a top driver in 2016 took home $6.5 million to $7 million a year in salary along with, $2 million in guaranteed prize money, a $500,000 to $1 million signing bonus and a personal services contract with the manufacturer or sponsor of $400,000 to $500,000.

In addition, RJR funded the NASCAR Winston Cup Leader Bonus from 1996 through 2003. It went to any driver who wins a race and, in the process, took the lead in the standings or maintained it. The jackpot started at $10,000 and increased each week no one wins. Overall, $360,000 a year was distributed, either to the winning driver or to the top 10 drivers at the end of the year.

Jeff Gordon received almost $1 million from the fund in his career to top all drivers. The largest jackpot, $310,000, went unclaimed at Homestead-Miami Speedway in 2002 and was distributed among the leading drivers.

Eventually, RJR reportedly paid out more than $100 million to drivers through its various bonus programs.

One of the more popular was the Winston Million. Bill Elliott was the initial driver to cash in when he captured three of four designated races in 1985 to take home $1 million the first year the program was offered. Jeff Gordon replicated that feat in 1997, the last year of the program.

In 1998, RJR started the No Bull Five, in which a driver who finished in the top five in a designated race won $1 million if he captured the next designated race. Fans were matched up with drivers and could win a matching bonus, too.

By the time the program ended at the close of the 2002 season, 13 drivers had cashed checks in 25 different opportunities.

All the money flowing into NASCAR altered the public perception of the sport. The annual banquet was moved to New York in 1981 to emphasize growing prestige and importance. It was an odd mix at first. The maitre d' at "21" tried to put a necktie on Junior Johnson, the man who helped bring RJR and NASCAR together. He stalked out and ate a hotdog on the street.

Today, the event is held in Las Vegas and is televised nationally with all the pomp of the Oscars. Drivers are media savvy and articulate, important American heroes on par with athletes in every major sport.

"Who thought in 1971 the sport would be where it is today?" RJR's Robertson said in 1985, but could have been talking about 2015. "I think we knew we were onto a good thing ... when RJR and NASCAR struck that first agreement, but I am not sure anyone could see just how big and popular this series would be ..."

Attendance boomed; so did the economic impact on Daytona Beach.

In 1973, the first Speedweeks with RJR involvement, *The Daytona Beach News-Journal* reported beachside motels were posting 30 percent gains in business compared to the previous year. A record crowd of 103,000 people showed up. By 1975, a year that endured a national economic downturn, business in Daytona Beach was up an estimated 20 percent compared to 1974 — when the gasoline shortage had curtailed travel.

"You can't imagine what this racing program means to this area," an anonymous Chamber of Commerce official told *The News-Journal* that year. "With the economy what it is elsewhere, we're fortunate indeed."

As the newspaper noted while reporting on the economic boon, "it looks like they've barely scratched the surface of this bonanza."

It worked for RJR, too, for 33 years. Legal scholar Alan Blum noted: "Winston Cup racing was unquestionably the most cost-effective campaign in advertising history. No brand of any product got more mileage at a cheaper rate than RJR did with NASCAR."[1]

No sponsor that has followed RJR Reynolds achieved the same level of return. After all, by the time tobacco left stock car racing, there was little left for Nextel, Sprint or Monster Energy to do.

CHAPTER 6: 1979
THE INTRODUCTION OF TELEVISION

The existence of the Speedway and the promotional push given by RJR attracted the attention of television, the world's biggest publicity agent.

That medium has a ferocious appetite. It needs to be fed 24 hours a day. Sports have been a natural part of the diet, but car racing was not typically on the menu. The three major networks in the 1960s — ABC, CBS and NBC — were all aware that racing existed. No executives, however, thought the sport had a national constituency.

That wasn't the first time a sport was downplayed by the electronic media. Just as ESPN started in 1978 by broadcasting obscure sports like Australian football (kind of a cross between rugby and soccer), networks tiptoed into the sports arena. They faced hostile team owners who were convinced that television would stop spectators from attending games. Baseball, the first sport to be televised extensively, battled against television's intrusion until surveys showed that publicity helped boost attendance.

By 1960, football and baseball were television staples. Coverage of motor, however, was limited to the Indianapolis 500 until January 31, 1960, when CBS decided to broadcast live the two

100-mile Daytona qualifying races (now the Gatorade 150s) and a couple of compact car events. An estimated 50 technicians flew in from New York to handle the two-hour *CBS Sports Spectacular* program. Considering that most race-related news was rarely mentioned in a newspaper, CBS was taking a very ambitious move. An estimated 17 million viewers tuned in as veteran newscaster Bud Palmer described the action.

CBS was apparently worried about its audience's attention span: the 100-mile qualifying races are less than an hour each, while the two compact car races lasted together less than 50 minutes. The Daytona 500 was considered too long to be broadcast, so the technicians left town 14 days before that year's "Great American Race," then just in its second year.

Less than two weeks later, NBC got into the act with a tape-delayed broadcast of a special 10-mile invitation-only race. It ran on the *Today* show and lasted less than five minutes. Ironically, Johnny Beauchamp won by inches over Ned Jarrett. In 1959, Beauchamp lost the inaugural Daytona 500 by the same margin to Lee Petty.

Despite signs of modest public enthusiasm, networks were not ready to make a commitment. Tapes of races were continually edited down to highlights for use on weekend sports anthologies, like the *ABC Wide World of Sports*, which began to include racing segments of the Firecracker 250 from Daytona Beach in 1961 as part of its "Wide World of Sports" program.

A race actually turned out to be ideal for television. With judicious editing, the action could seem continuous with plenty of room for commercials.

Separately, in 1971, TelePrompTer, then the largest cable company, which was not much of a distinction in those years, produced a live broadcast of the Daytona 500 with 12 cameras, slow motion and track-side interviews. However, only theatergoers were able to enjoy the action.

By 1970, ABC had taken the lead and started live broadcasts of several NASCAR races, always joining the selected event in progress. A year later, CBS went one step further and broadcast live from start to finish the Greenville 200 from a .5-mile, paved track in Greenville, South Carolina. Bobby Isaac won — his fourth straight win at that track — in an average time of 78.159 mph. That was a speed almost every viewer could relate to.

Soon after, ABC broadcast the entire Indianapolis 500 on tape delay. The Daytona 500 was not accorded the same respect. After all, the Indianapolis race was first held in 1911 and had built up years of history and prestige. So, only the last 200 miles or so of the Daytona 500 was broadcast live. In 1974, NASCAR was paid $300,000 for the privilege.

A year later, CBS ponied up $650,000 for the rights to broadcast five NASCAR races in the biggest motorsports contract to date. However, the Coca-Cola 600, which still runs the same day as the Indianapolis 500, and the Winston 500 from Talladega were still consigned to tape delay. ABC did broadcast the Daytona 500 that year, but only the start and finish of the race. In the middle, the network shifted to the Winter Olympics in Innsbruck, Austria.

Still, ABC attracted 19.5 million viewers for a 12.9 Nielsen rating. That lagged other comparative events, like the Super Bowl or the World Series, but still represented an impressive total.

Bill France recognized what adding televised events meant to the sport. "Not only is added televising of NASCAR races a boon for the sport itself, but it will be highly attractive to sponsors of racing teams at a time when exposure for them is most needed," he said.

France wasn't kidding. That year, NASCAR ran 30 races. They were won by only eight drivers: David Pearson and Cale

Yarborough each won eight times. Few other teams had the money to compete on an equal basis. As Bennie Parsons noted in 1978, a lament that was appropriate for almost any year in the 1970s, despite the influx of RJR cash, his budget for a one-drive team was $500,000, but his earnings only reached $312,000. Moreover, 20 of the 1976 races did not have a title sponsor.

Bill France commented about the financial strain: "A football lasts a whole season. Connecting rods, crankshafts and valves don't."

That year, however, NASCAR's Winston Cup Series moved into the top spot in worldwide motor sports attendance for the first time. "An estimated 1.4 million spectators making their way to events, according to figures from the Goodyear Tire and Rubber Company. That lead never has been relinquished." [1]

Eying those attractive numbers, CBS outbid ABC for the rights to broadcast the Daytona 500 live from green flag to checkered flag. The five-year contract came with an estimated $5 million price tag and was set to start in 1979. [2]

Barry Frank, senior vice president-CBS Sports, told reporters that airing the race "assures CBS of a strong viewing audience. It is the gemstone of our major auto racing package."

For the late Chris Economaki, the long-time voice of racing and a nationally renowned sports columnist, CBS' decision to buy the rights showed that racing was now seen as an equal with "major sporting events like the Olympics, the Kentucky Derby and the World Series ..." and added "significance and prestige (to) the televised event ..."

The network also taped other races held that same weekend and broadcast all but one prior to the Daytona 500. The lone exception was the ARCA race won by Kyle Petty, Richard's son and the subject of widespread interest and hype prior to the event. ARCA, founded by an associate of France, John Marcum, promoted stock car racing in the Midwest and still competes annually at Daytona International Speedway during Speedweeks. Marking the young Petty's debut into racing, the victory was the first by a third-generation athlete in any national sport. Reflecting its narrow perspective at the time, however, CBS didn't broadcast the tape of the race until April 28.

Fortunately for NASCAR, the cameras were filled with live action when the cars rolled off to start the 1979 Daytona 500, perhaps the most significant race in NASCAR history. It lasted nearly four hours and featured a top-notch field on an overcast, dreary afternoon, including rookies Dale Earnhardt, Geoffrey Bodine and Harry Gant, all of whom would enjoy Hall of Fame careers. They weren't household names then.

What created racing history took place after the checkered flag. With one lap to go, Donnie Allison held the lead. He was struggling to keep his No. 1 Hawaiian Tropic Oldsmobile under control at 200 mph and stay ahead of Cale Yarborough, the defending series champ who was inches behind in his No. 11 Busch Oldsmobile. Allison led the most of the day, clicking off the 2.5-mile laps at about 45 seconds each. With the end in sight, the starter showed the drivers the white flag, indicating one lap (2.5 miles) left to go.

Richard Petty, the sports' most famous driver, was in third, far back, and competing with Darrell Waltrip for that spot. Both drivers had lost cylinders in their engines and were falling further back with each passing mile. With them was A.J. Foyt, the Indianapolis 500 star who occasionally drove in the top stock car series.

Allison stayed low, the short way around the famed track, with Yarborough climbing the steep banking in turn 3 to Allison's right. Yarborough was famous for pulling up close behind a lead car, then using the draft to cut around in what was called a "slingshot" maneuver. With time running out, he dropped down and tried to go inside of Allison.

"I made up my mind that he would have to pass me up high," Allison said. "When he tried to pass me low, he went off the track. He spun and hit me. The track was mine until he hit me in the back. He got me loose and sideways, so I came back to get what was mine. He wrecked me; I didn't wreck him."

Actually, replays seem to show that Allison pinched Yarborough's Olds down to the apron, and Yarborough refused to hit his brakes. "He crashed me; it's as simple as that," Yarborough said. "I was going to pass him and win the race, but he turned left and crashed me. So, hell, I crashed him back. If I wasn't going to get back around, he wasn't either."

The cars rubbed together several times before a hard collision sent both up the banking into the outside wall in turn 3. The cars glanced off the concrete before coming to rest in the infield.

Ken Squier, broadcasting the race for CBS Sports, described the action: "It all comes down to this! Out of turn 3, Donnie Allison in first! Where will Cale make his move? He comes to the inside! Donnie Allison throws the block! Cale hits him! He slides! Donnie Allison slides! They hit again! They drive into the turn! They're hitting the wall! They're head-on in the wall! They slide to the inside! They're out of it!"

In his car, Petty saw the yellow caution light go on. By 2004, drivers were no longer allowed to change positions during a caution. In 1979, however, rules required drivers to race back to the start/finish line.

"Richard was jumping up and down in his seat," Waltrip said, describing Petty's reaction when they zoomed past the accident site.

Petty eventually outsprinted Waltrip and Foyt for the trophy. Foyt claimed he briefly checked up, an ingrained habit from his

Indianapolis 500 racing days when an accident froze the remaining drivers in place.

"Petty's win is not the big news that day," columnist Scott Oldham wrote. "His victory (did) not change the sport of stock car racing forever." What happened behind Victory Lane did.

The camera shifted quickly away from Petty crossing the finish line back to the damaged cars lying in the soggy infield. Neither Allison, who was credited with fourth place, nor Yarborough, listed as fifth in the official results, was injured in the accident. Dazed and dirty, both emerged slowly from their battered racing machines.

Yarborough was upset and frustrated. He had picked up several lost laps during a long and exhausting race to the checkered flag. He also thought Bobby Allison, Donnie's brother, had tried to block him just prior to the attempt at the last-lap pass. Yarborough was wrong about Bobby. Midway through the last lap, Yarborough and Donnie had actually come up on the lapped Ford of Ralph Jones, who was just trying to get out of their way by staying on the inside lane. Jones and Bobby Allison were both running white paint schemes that day, and Yarborough confused the two competitors. He wouldn't learn about his error until later.

Yarborough also thought Donnie should have given him room to make the pass; and, of course, he had just lost the Daytona 500. Eventually, he would win four of these races. Donnie Allison never came closer to taking home the checkered flag in the Daytona 500.

As a result, after jawing with Donnie, Yarborough was downright infuriated when Bobby cruised around the track and pulled to a stop near the damaged cars. Yarborough and Bobby yelled insults at each other. Then, Yarborough, helmet in hand, took a swing at Bobby through the car window.

Donnie tried to hold Yarborough as Bobby emerged from his

car. The three men started throwing punches and kicks. Bobby dove for Yarborough's legs, and, later in the confrontation, actually put his left hand on Yarborough's throat. Pictures show the two of them wrestling before officials stepped in to separate them. Yarborough then swapped angry retorts with Donnie for several minutes.

"Yeah, I was upset," Yarborough said years later. "But, it wasn't a fistfight. It was a little shoving match. But, it should have been a fight."

Captured on videotape, both men clearly are throwing punches, but none landed. The melee is quickly halted anyway by track officials who were already on their way to see if anyone was hurt in the accident.

All of that took place live, in the homes of millions of viewers.

"The brawl was over before it really started," Oldham continued. "But by the next morning at water coolers all over America, word was out that the Allisons and Yarborough had been involved in a full-on punch-out. The crash and the scuffle lit a flame of popularity under NASCAR that is still burning hot today .... Last-lap crashes were nothing new. Neither were infield fights. So why did that race create such an impact? Television. It was the first time a network covered the Daytona 500, or any NASCAR race, live from flag to flag. And, it was the first use of the now-ubiquitous in-car camera, which was mounted in Benny Parson's car. Most importantly, those CBS cameras captured every second of that dramatic finish, including the post-race brawl. February 18, 1979, was the day much of America, including Madison Avenue, discovered NASCAR."

"Nobody knew it then, but that was the race that got everything going," said Dick Berggren, a Motor Racing Network announcer that day. "It was the first 'water cooler' race, the first time people had stood around water coolers on Monday and talked about seeing a race on TV the day before. It took a while — years, maybe — to realize how important it was." [3]

The impact was actually swifter than that. Fans loved it. Television ratings for the Daytona 500 topped 10. 4 percent, a race record that stood until 2002 (10.9). Each rating point then represented about 1.05 million households. Sports events on rival networks — golf and a boxing match — were largely ignored.

"We were very, very pleased," said Beano Cook, a CBS commentator.

The show would also win an Emmy Award.

Later, Bill France was asked if he was going to fine the brawlers. "Fine them?" France said in disbelief. "Hell, I might give them a raise."

NASCAR and CBS had been lucky — a snow storm in the Northeast had forced many people to stay home and watch television. On the other hand, the drama of the race coupled with the extra curricular activities had generated a surge of interest. Calls and ticket sales at the next race on the circuit — at Rockingham, North Carolina — shot up.

"We're getting inquiries about tickets from people, who in the gist of their conversation and questions, obviously weren't interested in racing previously," reported Frank Wilson, vice president of the track. "They have to be the people who were attracted by what they saw on TV."

When ESPN opened its doors, it needed something to compete with NFL games on Sunday afternoon. NASCAR was cheap and filled the empty space. In 1981, ESPN and NASCAR hit the airwaves together. By 1984, ESPN was broadcasting 63 NASCAR races annually, including 12 in the Winston Cup Series.

In 1984, CBS again placed a camera inside a stock car. "Suddenly the TV audience could see what the driver sees and hear every boom and shrieking twist of metal," one writer noted. "It's fun to watch a flock of cars beetle around a track from above, but it isn't until you get to ride with the drivers that the brutal, rock-et-sled-on-rails experience becomes addictive." [4] ESPN installed a foot cam to show Ricky Rudd's footwork during a race on a road course and a bumper cam to show how close drivers actually came to each other.

The racing was fierce. "Hollywood scriptwriters couldn't have come up with this stuff. When you look back at the 1980s ... the names, the characters and the stories are just phenomenal. Talk about the ultimate male soap opera," said Patti Wheeler, who served as director of TNN (now Spike TV) Motorsports in the 1990s.

Women also were interested. Studies in the 1990s found that half of the race audience was female. "Women drive cars, too," Wheeler pointed out. "We don't play football; we drive cars."

That revelation drew retailers who had ignored racing. Tide and Folgers coffee both saw sales boom when they sponsored drivers. When McDonald's dropped fan favorite Bill Elliott, sales plummeted. The company quickly resumed sponsoring race cars.

By 1990, 24 races in NASCAR's elite series aired on cable television ESPN, TNN and TBS. ESPN bought heavily into NASCAR since it couldn't afford rights to other major sports. As a result, the number of televised races reached 28 races by the end of the decade. Then, in 2001, NASCAR scored an incredible coupe. Previously, tracks negotiated individual television contracts. NASCAR assumed the rights, creating an enormous package that drew FOX/NBC and ousted ESPN.

The two networks agreed to pay NASCAR $2.4 billion for eight years for the broadcast rights to the 34-race annual NASCAR Winston (now Sprint) Cup Series. In 2013, FOX and NBC signed a 10-year $8.2 billion contract to broadcast races. That contract placed stock car racing on par with professional football and basketball. The National Football League has started a $4.95 billion contract that runs from 2015 through 2021. The NBA is getting $2.6 billion from 2016 through 2025, while Major League Baseball earns $1.5 billion from a 7-year contract that started in 2014.

Starting in 2006, every NASCAR race in its three national touring series has been televised on NBC, TNT, FOX or the SPEED Channel. The viewing audience dwarfs almost every other program. Nielsen Media Research, which reported that 189 million households tuned in to watch NASCAR's premier series in 2003 — a 58 percent gain over the 120 million households that tuned in during the 2000 season. That audience reached 5.1 million viewers across FOX, Fox Sports 1, NBC and NBCSN in 2015, according to Sports Business Daily. However, that total represents a drop of 4 percent from 2014 and 12 percent from 2013, according to Sports Business.

In contrast, Major League Baseball touted an average of 2.2 million viewers in 2015, up 16 percent from a record-low 1.9 million viewers in 2014, but below the 2.4 million average viewers in 2013. The numbers for basketball are worse. The NBA on TNT averaged 1.67 million viewers in 2015, the lowest figure since the 2007-08 season. Overall, viewership fell 12 percent from 2013 levels.

NASCAR's hefty audience also indicates how televised events helped change cultural biases about racing.

"Television made it OK to go to a race," explained motor sports media legend Economaki in 1998. "For years, it wasn't."

Once television placed racing on equal footing with other major American sports, it created a multiple of side benefits.

After the 1979 race, interest climbed especially when movie producers realized that car races offered opportunities for spectacular crashes along with human drama. The marriage of medium and sport remains strong. The link to Hollywood has been enhanced over the years by movies, including Will Farrell's *Talladega Nights: The Ballad of Ricky Bobby*, Tom Cruise's *Days of Thunder* and the cartoon *Cars* along with dozens more. At the same time, drivers began making guest appearances on such TV shows as *Wheel of Fortune*, *Pyramid* and *Who Wants To Be a Millionaire.*

Another big effort came in 2004 with the opening of *NASCAR 3D: The IMAX Experience®* in select IMAX® Theaters around the country.

According to a company publicity announcement, "Through a partnership of Warner Bros. Pictures, NASCAR Digital Entertainment, IMAX Corporation and AOL for Broadband, *NASCAR 3D: The IMAX Experience* introduces viewers to the heart-pounding thrills of NASCAR and puts them in the driver's seat through the magic of IMAX 3D technology, brought to life on screens up to eight stories tall with 12,000 watts of digital surround sound."

Paul Brooks, senior vice president, NASCAR, was enthusiastic about the film. "People start to understand the magic of our sport when they attend their first NASCAR race in person where the intense drama, sound, emotion, thrills and excitement of NASCAR can be experienced firsthand on our incredible real-life stage," he said. "This film will allow us to immerse an audience in the NASCAR experience at IMAX theaters worldwide and attract new fans to the sport, while bringing tremendous exposure and value to our drivers, teams, tracks, sponsors and other partners."

The movie connections did not happen by chance. NASCAR makes sure the links remain forged with dollar bills. NASCAR remains the only sports organization to place lobbyists in Los Angeles where the staff located in the heart of the entertainment industry busily promotes the sport.

The man who suggested creating the office is Brian Z. France, the grandson of the founder and who, in September 2003, became NASCAR's chairman and CEO.

Brooks, who oversees the company's entertainment interests, told *The News-Journal* that wooing Hollywood was a key strategy in growing the sport.

"We wanted to grow further and knew getting involved in the entertainment community through films, television and music would be a way to reach new audiences," he said.

In return, drivers have become integrated into American culture. At one time, only a few drivers could hope to commercial endorsements. Richard Petty, for example, was spokesman for STP and Goody's headache powders. Other drivers might show up in ads for a particular car battery or similar products.

These days, a top driver like four-time NASCAR Sprint Cup champion Jeff Gordon has plenty of gigs outside his new role as a TV commentator, including appearing in ads and in TV shows. He previously hosted *Saturday Night Live* in January 2003 and made a cameo appearance in a 2003 "Looney Tunes" movie.

Dale Earnhardt Jr., who hopped on stage at Watkins Glen International in 2001 to join a band playing in a pre-race concert there, has appeared in several music videos, including Sheryl Crow's "Steve McQueen" video. "It's fun for me because I love music of all kinds," Earnhardt Jr. said in a story in the *Daytona Beach News-Journal*. "I think more and more musicians are kind of discovering NASCAR and really enjoy it, so it gives me a chance to meet people I enjoy listening to."

The son of NASCAR icon Dale Earnhardt, the North Carolinian is long been the most popular driver in racing's elite stock car series and has been the subject of two shows on MTV: a one-hour documentary of the 2000 season called *True Life*; and *Cribs*, which tours the home of celebrities. "Little E" was also a presenter on the 2001 MTV Music Video Awards show besides serving as a

TC spokesman for several companies.

NASCAR's influence extends beyond a few divers who land commercials. Actor Arnold Schwarzenegger, then thinking of running for governor of California, served as an honorary official at California Speedway in 2003, for example. He was plugging a movie, of course. Other feature films have been given an extra push by painting images on race cars.

Long outside the general culture, NASCAR has longed to become accepted on the same level of other major sports. For starters, celebrities followed the cameras. Bill France would not have been surprised by the interest. He worked long hours trying to seduce celebrities into visiting Daytona Beach for the races. He enjoyed modest success.

From 1959 through the 1970s, the only celebrities were race fans like Presidents Jimmy Carter, Reagan and George H. G. and George W. Bush, and Alabama Governor George Wallace. France was a Republican; Wallace a Democrat, but that didn't matter in the world of publicity, nor did Wallace's controversial racial views.

Celebrities were attracted, too, but only if they had some interest in racing from a personal or financial standpoint. They always caused a small stir, at least among the local media.

In 1970, actress Joan Crawford came by Daytona International Speedway on behalf of Pepsi to watch the race, won by Pete Hamilton. Writer Tom Tucker described her visit this way: "Crawford, who dines on caviar with kings, presidents, celluloid heroes and giants of a fading era, watches Hamilton, who eats hamburgers sitting on a stack of worn out tires with Maurice and Richard Petty, kings of the era of today, and the future. Both, heroes of two different worlds, were in Daytona International Speedway Sunday, doing their thing. The attraction was the Daytona 500 miler stock car race."

Two years later, the late King Hussein of Jordan made a surprise visit under heavy security, telling *News-Journal* sports editor, Bernard Kahn, "At Daytona Beach, I am a fan. I've always liked fast competition and am enthusiastic about racing."

Hussein was drawn to Daytona Beach because he drove in a variety of hill climbs, rallies and related events in his own country.

George H.W. Bush showed up twice to serve as an honorary official: 1978, when he headed the CIA; and, again in 1983 as vice president.

Everything is different now. The merger of racing and Hollywood took a "significant step forward" in 2001, according to *The News-Journal*'s Godwin Kelly when pop diva Britney Spears came to Daytona for the Pepsi 400.

"From that point," he wrote, "this showbiz-racing snowball has gained incredible momentum."

Naturally, she came to Florida for business reasons. Spears was the Pepsi spokesperson then. Her impact on stock car racing, however, stretched far beyond a single soft drink company.

Gillian Zucker, now president of business operations for the NBA's San Diego Clippers, told *The News-Journal*, "Britney was the person who got us to the next level. She came to Daytona through our relationship with Pepsi. But once you get a star of that caliber and people see the kind of exposure they'll get, it's much easier to make a case to others."

It doesn't hurt that the Daytona 500 is the most watched motor sports event in the United States. That kind of attention works like a magnet. During 2003 Speedweeks, for example, actor John Travolta gave a stirring command to the drivers to start their engines as the Grand Marshal for the 45th running of "The Great American Race," while Grammy Award winning artist Mariah Carey, the biggest-selling female pop artist of all time, sang the national anthem and waved the green flag to get historic race underway.

Also in attendance at "The World Center of Racing" for the Daytona 500 that year were tennis ace Serena Williams, skateboarding icon Tony Hawk, American Idol judge Randy Jackson, action movie superstar Vin Diesel, boxing champion Evander Holyfield and Travolta's wife/actress Kelly Preston. Two-time Emmy-nominated comic actor Wayne Brady performed at the exclusive Grand Marshal's dinner.

"The problem having an actor as a Grand Marshal is he only has one line. I haven't had only one line in 30 years," Travolta quipped, referring to the command "Gentlemen, start your engines."

Travolta was not necessarily coming here to boost his career. As a seasoned pilot, he has a yen for speed. He is also former Daytona Beach area resident, moving out only after neighbors at the Spruce Creek Fly-In — where residents can taxi up to their own front doors and park in garage-hangars — objected to the size of his aircraft.

"It's like being home again," Travolta said. "When I lived here, I used to come every year to the Pepsi 400 or the Daytona 500. It was pretty exciting."

He was following almost as many footprints as there are handprints in concrete in front of Grumman's Chinese Theater in Hollywood.

Entertainers like James Garner, Lily Tomlin, Roy Rogers and Ben Gazarra have all been here during Speedweeks. Supreme Court Justice Clarence Thomas presided as Grand Marshal over the 1999 Daytona 500. Other celebrities in the crowd have included Jay Leno, Kelly Clarkson, Nicolas Cage and Vanessa Williams.

Actor Ben Affleck was invited to be the grand marshal for the 2004 Daytona 500 — he was relocated to the pace car when

President George W. Bush decided to rev up his re-election campaign by coming the race — after Zucker saw him pictured in a magazine wearing a No. 29 Kevin Harvick NASCAR hat. "I ripped that page out and brought it to work that day, and found out who was his publicist and called their office," she explained. Afflack agreed quickly. No appearance fee was offered or asked for.

It was not a hard sell.

"They know the Daytona 500 is an international event," Zucker said. "They know it will be seen in more than 100 countries and broadcast in 20 languages. The fact we're able to secure stars of that caliber without providing any payment says what they're seeing is that it's a major benefit for them to be involved in the event."

There were plenty by the mid-1960s. NASCAR drivers competed in as many as 64 a year. After the start of the Modern Era in 1972, the number dropped into the low 30s, but the season stretched longer than in any other major sport — February through November. The major race of the year, the Daytona 500, was televised. Sponsors were creeping into the sport, although only a handful of teams actually could compete on an equal basis.

The sport only had one drawback — *prestige.*

There was little.

The media largely ignored stock car racing along with the bulk of the public. Attendance may have topped 1.5 million people at all NASCAR Sprint Cup races in the early 1980s, but that was a good annual gate for a single baseball team. Reports of races were typically limited to a single paragraph in a roundup of "other" events. Drivers like Mario Andretti, A.J. Foyt, Johnny Rutherford, Bobby Rahal and Al Unser held the public attention for their Indianapolis 500 exploits, not for their success in stock cars, even though Foyt and Andretti both won the Daytona 500. By doing so, they effectively demonstrated the superiority of Indy drivers. After all, Andretti rarely competed in stock cars and won the only NASCAR race he entered.

Bill France and other NASCAR honchos realized that they needed to increase the status of NASCAR drivers to achieve complete parity with other sports on the national stage. As a result of television and the efforts of RJR Reynolds, the sport was better known, but the drivers were still viewed largely as illiterate moonshiners from the backwoods.

In an effort to place stock car racers on the same footing with the Indy stars, two leaders in the sport came up with an all-star event gaudily named the International Race of Champions. Les Richter, a former National Football League lineman, and car builder/owner Roger Penske figured fans would turn out to see which drivers were better. They were wrong. The four-race series has never attracted much interest and has almost folded at least three times in its 26 years of existence, before disbanding in 2007.

Nevertheless, IROC eventually succeeded in demonstrating that NASCAR drivers possessed superior skills. For the first IROC edition in 1973, three drivers were invited from each of four major motor sports' arenas: USAC, NASCAR, SCCA, and Formula 1. Driving identical Porsche Carrera RSR cars, they competed in three races on Riverside (California) International Raceway's road course in October. Four months later, the top six then raced in the finale on Daytona International Speedway's road course. Mark Donohue, who eventually drove in all four-race series but was then representing SCCA, won three of the races and the series.

The advantage to NASCAR, however, was that, for the first time, its drivers competed as equals with competitors from other series. Over time, Bill France Jr., who took control of NASCAR from his dad in 1972, rigged the deck to give his stock car aces an edge. As a result, IROC competed only on oval tracks in stock cars — typically Pontiac Firebirds — with only a handful of Indy drivers in the field. At that time, Indy drivers rarely saw an oval, but more often raced on city streets.

Given that edge, the last IROC champion from the open-wheel division was Al Unser Jr. in 1983. Stock car drivers won most of the annual races anyway.

That success failed to boost stock car racing's reputation enough. For that, France needed a lot more. He needed star power. However, few celebrities competed in motor sports events. Someone like Kevin Costner can tout baseball, while numerous football players can easily shift into movies and TV, including Alex Karras, Jim Brown, Burt Reynolds and Dwayne Johnson, motorsports could count participating celebrities on one hand.

Singer Marty Robbins drove in 35 NASCAR stock car races over 13 years, and never finished higher than 48th. Robbins crashed so often that he was nicknamed "NASCAR's official wall tester." He did so well in one race that he asked NASCAR officials to check the engine. Naturally, they found evidence of cheating and disqualified him.

The late actor Paul Newman drove in road races, although he tried to stay out of the limelight. He also achieved some success. At age 70, he became the oldest competitor to win a sanctioned race when his team captured the 24 Hours of Daytona in 1995.

Buz McKim, the NASCAR Hall of Fame archivist, spent some time trying to think of any other "name" performers who drove in races, but gave up.

NASCAR finally got a break in 1970 when Georgia native Jimmy Carter ran for governor in his home state. He promised a barbecue dinner in the governor's mansion for drivers and sponsors if he won the seat, and followed through after the election. An avid race fan and former ticket vendor at Atlanta Motor

Speedway in the 1960s, Carter won the presidency in 1976, defeating incumbent Gerald Ford, then brought the racing community to the White House in 1978 for another cookout.

Several race cars were parked on the front lawn for display. Carter's wife, Rosalyn, asked Richard Petty to start his. Petty declined politely, saying the engine was very loud. The First Lady insisted. The resulting roar reportedly rattled dishes in the White House kitchen.

France could only hope to have the same effect on media, which saw Carter's stock car enthusiasm as an object of derision.

He got his wish. In 1984, only four years after stock car racing's biggest fan left office, one race changed the public perception of stock car racing. That race literally launched the sport from beyond its secure southern roots into the national consciousness. Television introduced the sport; this race lifted it to major status.

CHAPTER 7: 1984

REAGAN'S VISIT TO STOCK CAR RACES

On July 4 that year, the world finally came to stock car racing, led by an affable former actor who occupied the White House. President Ronald Reagan startled everyone by agreeing to be the grand marshal for the 1984 Firecracker 400, the summer race at Daytona.

No one has ever explained why he wanted to come or who made the invitation. Reagan may have simply decided to visit as part of a tough re-election campaign against Massachusetts' Walter Mondale. The election would turn out to be a rout, but Reagan couldn't see into the future. He and his political strategists did know that NASCAR fans represented the conservative wing of the country. The campaign openly catered to them by purchasing a small share of the sponsorship of the car driven by Steve Moore, who only competed in a limited number of NASCAR races that year.

Reagan may also have wanted to become part of sports history. After all, while living in Des Moines, Iowa in the 1930s, he had been a sports announcer. He did understand sports and their social importance, and had probably heard the murmurs about this particular event.

The Firecracker 400 that year was special. Five weeks before

Daytona's race, Petty, the son of a Hall of Fame driver and father of another racer, had won the 199th NASCAR Winston Cup Series race of his career. No one had ever won 200 races in any sanctioned motorsports series. The next closest driver to Petty on the NASCAR victory list was David Pearson, who retired in the late 1980s with 105 checkered flags. Most drivers simply did not compete long enough to pile up numbers like that. Petty started early and had been racing in the top NASCAR series since 1958, usually against inferior competition. He had money, a sponsor and the best equipment money could conjure. And, he was extremely talented with charisma, an affectionate grin and an easy manner with adoring fans. That combination had crowned him the "king" of stock car racing.

By 1984, Petty was on the downside of his spectacular career. He turned 47 two days before the Firecracker 400, an elder statesman in a sport that demands the lightning reflexes and the stamina of a young man. He won at Dover Downs (Delaware) International Speedway five weeks before Daytona, then struggled, finishing 34, 23, 13 and 34 in successive races. Mechanical problems knocked him out of two of the four events.

Still, Petty thought he had a chance at Daytona where he had won a record seven Daytona 500s. So did his fellow competitors.

"I think everybody was talking about his 200th win, but everybody was also thinking about not letting him get it, too," said rival Cale Yarborough, who sat in the pole position for the 1984 Firecracker 400. "I didn't have a problem with it. I didn't want him to have it either. I wanted it."

Drivers were not the only ones talking about Petty's drive for the record book.

Reagan and the possible 200th win dominated the conversation all week prior to the race, according to announcer Barney Hall.

"There was a lot of excitement in the garage area that President Reagan was going to be down there," Hall said. "That pretty much dominated the conversation for the better part of the week down there. The only cat that was pretty laid back about it all was Richard. The press was bugging him all week, and he was as cool as a cucumber." Hall felt that Petty was viewed as one of the race favorites. "There wasn't any question about that," he said. "Everybody knew how much they had worked to get a car capable of getting him his 200th win at Daytona. And, Daytona had been his cup of tea for years. He won so many races there. If there was a place he was likely to break his 200th deal, it was Daytona. Everybody felt that way — Richard and his team and the other drivers." [1]

Reagan declined to get drawn into the speculation. Asked Chris Economaki who he was rooting for, the president responded, "I'm pulling for them all. Yet I know that only one can win, and I'm the only one who knows who that is, so I'm going to keep it a secret." Not too secret. Reagan wore a cap with Petty's famed STP logo on it. [2]

Petty started sixth in the 42-car field. Back in 35th was Moore, with "Reagan in '84" painted on his car's hood. Ken Ragan was in 24th with a sign on the back of his car that read "Ragan's for Reagan."

But, Reagan wasn't there to appreciate the sentiment. Instead, notoriously late for most of his appointments, he was still flying into town on Air Force One when the drivers lined up in pit row to begin the race. Using a telephone hookup in the plane, he gave the official order: "Gentlemen, start your engines."

It was 10 a.m. The Florida sun is brutal during the summer. Thundershowers invariably pop up in the afternoon. So, the July 4 race always began in the morning until moved under the lights in 1998. For drivers, the heat in the car could top 140 degrees.

As the race got underway, Reagan landed at Daytona International Speedway, which is located behind the backstretch. The big jet was clearly visible by the more than 100,000 people in the stands. (NASCAR still doesn't release attendance figures, but rarely sold all seats for the summer race in those days.)

In the early going, Petty clearly had the strongest car, but Yarborough stayed close. In stock car races, a car that's powerful early in the race can lose some of its aerodynamic advantage through tire wear or attempted improvements made by the pit crew. Sometimes, even a new set of tires can upset the delicate balance. As a result, drivers who lead the most laps are never guaranteed to win a race.

While Petty and Yarborough dueled, Reagan made his way into the radio broadcast booth. In his pre-movie days, the Illinois native had broadcast Chicago Cub baseball games via tickertape. He would read the tape and pretend he was at the game, a common technique for stations that covered sports, but which couldn't afford to send a reporter to actually watch the games.

He was on the microphone, chatting with announcer Ned Jarrett, as the race came to its climax. By then, Petty was in front.

Jarrett reported, "Going into turn 1, Cale Yarborough continues to gain on Richard Petty, so it looks like we'll have a shootout down near the end of this race between those two drivers. They pulled away from the balance of the field. Currently running in third place is Terry Labonte. Harry Gant is in fourth place and Bobby Allison in fifth place. And, a fellow who has put on more good races with Richard Petty, David Pearson, is pulling into the pits now — the hood goes up on that car, and there's trouble on the race track, Mr. President. We need to give it to our turn announcer."

There was a problem. Moore had scraped the wall. The race

continued unabated. Soon after, rookie Doug Heveron spun his No. 01 Chevrolet off the track in turn one. As Petty and Yarborough thundered past the start/finish line to begin lap 158, the yellow caution flag waved. These days, as noted earlier, cautions immediately freeze drivers into position for the next restart. The modern approach would have been to hold a green-white-checkered flag finish, but not then. Under the more recent rules, Petty would have coasted across the start/finish line. In 1984, he didn't have that luxury. That rule did not change until 2003. Until then, drivers raced back to the start/finish line. Whoever got there first took the lead when the caution ended.

There wouldn't have been enough laps left in 1984 to have a restart. As a result, Petty and Yarborough suddenly found themselves in a one-lap shootout for the victory.

"With three laps to go, we both seen a bunch of dust or something up in the air," Petty said. "We went past the start/finish line, and the caution came out. I knew I had to get back to the finish line first. Cale realized the same thing."

Petty also knew that Yarborough was hanging back in order to "slingshot" around him at the last moment.

"Cale was sitting back there waiting for the last lap, and I knew that," said Petty, who practically invented the "slingshot" maneuver.

The caution changed that strategy. Yarborough could not afford to wait. As they raced down the back straightaway of the 2.5-miles track, Yarborough passed Petty for the lead going into turn 3. His momentum carried him up the banking. Taking advantage of that move and the presence of two lapped cars that pulled low to allow the two competitors to fly by unimpeded, Petty immediately regained the lead.

"Richard picked up the draft off some slower cars exiting turn four and got ahead," Yarborough said. "Maybe those lapped cars wouldn't have been there for him to draft if the race had gone to lap 160."

Petty had another view and never mentioned the slower cars. "I got in there and got up beside him, and we raced back to the flag," he said.

Side by side, with the president gaping and fans on their feet, the two drivers touched at least three times as they exited turn 4 and came screaming through the final yards of the trioval.

Petty drifted up to force Yarborough higher. Yarborough steered his No. 28 Hardee's Chevrolet down to push Petty lower.

"The last bam squirted my car a little ahead," Petty said. "We touched a couple of times coming for the line; enough to affect the cars but not enough to upset them. I was on the inside of the track," he continued, "and he was on the outside. When we turned in the dogleg, he had to go three or four more foot than me, and that's how much I beat him by. From where I sat, I knew I had him. I didn't know if it was a foot or a yard or three yards or an inch. I just knew I had him. At that point, the margin didn't make no difference."

Officially, the winning distance was about two feet.

Yarborough was so befuddled by the loss, he dove into the pits instead of staying on the track for the final two laps. "I got beat at my own game," he said ruefully. He was placed third in the final standings by kindly NASCAR officials. "I was sitting right where I wanted to be, but a late caution isn't something you can anticipate."

Hall was calling the race for the Motor Racing Network (MRN), a media outlet France created in 1970 to get his races on the air. "It was so close I couldn't call it," he said. "I was excited as everybody else was when they came off turn 4 beating and banging. When they came across the line, I personally didn't think

Petty had won from the angle I was looking at it, but it turned out he did."[4]

Petty, who never won again before retiring in 1992, was escorted into Victory Lane, then up to Bill France's luxury loge in the Winston Tower to meet President Reagan. The veteran driver understood completely the significance of his victory.

"That race was the pinnacle of my career," Petty said in 2004 during the 20th anniversary of his historic victory. "Winning 200 anywhere would have been great, but doing it under those circumstances and beating Cale, who I'd been racing with for years — it was all in one day, and it was just fantastic.

"It still is. I don't think there's anything to match it in the annals of racing."

Reagan understood the situation as well. He joined an afternoon picnic in the infield and munched on chicken with the guests there.

"I've enjoyed certainly everything that I've seen since I've been here," he told them, according to the official White House transcript. "And with the skill and the daring that we witnessed out there, and the pursuit of excellence that those drivers ... made stock car racing a major American sport ... I think I can understand why stock car racing is so popular. Americans have always cherished mobility, and we greatly admire innovation. And by combining man and machine, stock car racing brings out the best of both of these American impulses."

Reagan exaggerated. Stock car racing was not a major American sport yet, but his presence helped propel it into the spotlight.

"Reagan's presence was a huge publicity lick for NASCAR, which was years from becoming accepted by the mainstream media," a veteran motorsports columnist noted. "France was quick to brag that Reagan chose the 400 from among his hundreds of options for an Independence Day getaway." [5]

The significance of the race was obvious to the media. "Many onlookers feel that Richard Petty winning his 200th victory in front of the president at Daytona International Speedway on July 4 is a turning point in the growth of NASCAR." [6]

More importantly, as Chris Economaki noted, "Reagan made it OK for average fans to go to stock car races."

Soon after, they started showing up in droves.

CHAPTER 8: 1992
YOUTH
SHOWS UP

By 1992, the sport was starting to languish again. Its biggest star, Richard Petty was 55 and unable to maintain the pace. He hadn't won a race in eight years. Other big names, like Cale Yarborough, Bobby Allison and David Pearson, had faded from the scene. In most cases, they simply lost rides, and no one would hire them. No other sport treats its long-time stars so shabbily. Baseball even developed the designated hitter so popular sluggers who had lost a step in the field could maintain a place in the game. Unlike drivers, basketball players are paid well enough that they can step away from the game gracefully. Hockey players, at least, can look forward to enshrinement in a hall of fame. They often get hired to coach, general manager or scout for various teams.

Stock car has several halls of fame; none carry a hint of prestige or draw the kind of attention given the other major sports. The new one in Charlotte has done nothing to change that attitude. Attendance is poor.

Options are limited. For example, there are no scouts in racing. Modern drivers, at least, banked millions. That wasn't true until the turn of the century. As a result, retired drivers who want to stay in the sport have only a couple choices. Some, like Buddy Baker, opened schools to teach drivers to nuances of races. Richard

Petty has a business letting ordinary people sit in a race car at close to full speed.

Former drivers who can scrounge up sufficient funds have tried to start their own teams with sufficient funds. Rick Hendrick, Richard Childress and Roger Penske successfully went that route, but many failed, including Cale Yarborough and Michael Waltrip.

As a result, many of the old-timers live in obscure near-poverty, returning to the situations they once tried to flee in a fast race car.

In 1992, the sport stood on a cusp: older drivers were fading away or gone. No one had seemed able to capture their mystique. Dale Earnhardt, the son of a driver, carried the weight of the sport, but even he could not do it alone.

Then came the 1992 Hooters 500 at Atlanta (Georgia) Motor Speedway. Caught up in the then-closest championship race in NASCAR history, six different drivers were mathematically capable of walking away with the title. The top three, Alan Kul-wicki, Davey Allison and Bill Elliott were separated by only a few points The trio swapped the lead through much of the year, helping maintain fan interest and national media attention.

Amid some very familiar names in the field, including Petty, Dale Earnhardt, Mark Martin, Harry Gant, Geoffrey Bodine and Darrell Waltrip, there was a youngster named Jeff Gordon who had garnered a hefty amount of publicity and some skeptical curiosity, but whose first NASCAR Sprint Cup race was eclipsed by the fact Petty was making his last start. Petty still drew legions of fans to the races and spent his final season on what was dubbed "The Fan Appreciation Tour."

Presumably, the fans enjoyed seeing his finish back in the pack every race. Darrell Waltrip tried the same routine a few years later and performed equally as dismally. Jeff Gordon was one of the few retiring drivers to have a decent year. In 2016, Tony Stewart injured his back and missed the season-opening Daytona 500 in perhaps the most miserable start to his goodbye tour.

Petty's last start was no better than his previous races: he started this race in 39th and end 35th. At least, his famous No. 43 STP Pontiac was still running when the checkered flag waved.

The Atlanta race has often been included among the greatest in NASCAR history. Allison, son of a legendary driver and the newest fan favorite, had the points lead going into the event, the 29th and final one of the year. Behind him in third was Elliott, who had won four in a row earlier in the year, and had left his own family team that season to drive for Junior Johnson. In between the two men was Alan Kulwicki, an independent driver who had to be considered a long shot. After all, teams were quickly becoming the norm in NASCAR. Kulwicki would become the last owner-driver to have a chance to win the championship until Tony Stewart matched that feat in 2011.

Allison, who only had to finish fifth to take the title, failed to complete the race. Ernie Irvan spun out and collected Allison's Ford on lap 88. Allison was credited with 27th place in the 41-car field.

Elliott's red No. 11 Budweiser Ford led early in the race, while Kulwicki in the No. 7 Hooters Ford stayed close behind. Kulwicki's crew chief, Paul Andrews, figured out that if his driver finished second and won the most laps, it wouldn't matter what Elliott did. Johnson had worked out the same formula, but was unable to tell Elliott because of a broken radio.

Everything came down to a single lap. Kulwicki survived a late-race mishap in the pits when his crew failed to get much gas into the tank and finished second behind Elliott. However, he won the five point bonus for leading the most laps and, as a result, the title.

Far behind the duo, Gordon finished in 31st place. A single-car accident on lap 71 ended his day. His result may have earned a line in some newspaper, perhaps back in his hometown of Vallejo, California.

Not much was expected of him anyway. He was only 21, the second youngest driver ever in a NASCAR race at that time. The youngest, Donald Thomas, brother of champion Herb Thomas, competed in 1952 and won a race and a pole that year at age 20. Since then, car owners had been banked on mature drivers, not a kid like Gordon, who at 5'7" and maybe 150 pound, looked incapable of wrestling with the huge cars or fending off the battle scarred veterans around him. He even grew a wispy mustache before the season in hopes of looking older. It didn't help.

He waved nervously to the crowd that day during driver introductions and settled into the No. 24 DuPont Chevrolet. "At that time," he said years later, "I just wanted to build a team that would gain experience and consistency. I didn't even know if I had what it took to win races in Winston Cup. When you get to this level, you know you're surrounded by the best. You know these guys are so good. You just don't know if you're good enough to be here, let alone win."[1]

The following February, he won one of the 125-mile races to qualify for the 1993 Daytona 500 and then the rookie of the year award. In 1994, he picked up his first checkered flag and began piling up victories, ending with the third-highest total in NASCAR history behind only Petty and Pearson.

"The theory prior to Jeff Gordon is that nobody started winning major, long- distance races in the U.S., whether that was in Winston Cup or the Indy Racing League, until they were about 28," said H.A. "Humpy "Wheeler, a long-time promoter and track owner. "Jeff Gordon came along and shot that theory down."[2]

In many cases, younger drivers did not have a chance to

succeed. Even a driver like Dale Jarrett, the son of a Hall of Fame driver, would start with a weak team, build up experience, and then finally be hired by one of the top teams and given a chance to run for the championship.

"Those of us who came along in the1980s, the owners weren't willing to put younger guys in the cars because they thought experience was what won races," Jarrett said. "I know that Dale Earnhardt never got to this level as quickly as Dale Earnhardt Jr. did. With each generation, things have been accelerated." [3]

Ricky Rudd, who once held the NASCAR Sprint Cup record with more than 700 consecutive starts, described the class warfare in the top series. He said new drivers started on a C team, then, if they showed any promise, moved to a B team. Finally, if an owner was impressed, the driver would get a chance with an A team.

"Years ago, when rookies would come in, they would be with teams that aren't on top of the list as far as the equipment and everything else like that," added two-time champion Terry Labonte. "When I ran my first race in Darlington, S.C., (in 1978), I set the car up myself and drove the truck down there. Years ago, that's how most people started out. There weren't the big teams. There were only a few top teams that won the races and had the established drivers, and everybody else was kind of in the same boat." [4]

These days, Labonte continued, "young drivers really have an opportunity to be with top-notch teams right from the start. Things have changed."

Gordon gets all the credit for that. He was only 22 when he won his first race and went on to capture four NASCAR Sprint Cup titles along with 93 Cup wins and 5 more in the Xfinity Series. But, he did more than win races. He revolutionized the sport off the track.

"Jeff has been one of those people who changed what a race car driver is. Look at Richard Petty. Look at Dale Earnhardt. Look at Cale Yarborough. Then look at Jeff Gordon. That's not the same picture. Jeff helped bring mainstream young America into our sport," said driver Jeff Burton on ESPN Classic's SportsCentury series.

Gordon actually smoothed the rumpled image of the entire sport.

"In years past, the circuit was nothing but gritty, slimy, bar-fighting guys who lived in the back of a pickup," said Gordon's stepfather, John Bickford. "[They] drank their breakfast and once they got on the track, just wanted to bang into each other." [5]

"There aren't too many good ol' boys left among the ranks of NASCAR drivers. Today's drivers are relatively polished because they have to sell themselves to buttoned-down executives. For that, much of the credit — or blame — goes to Jeff Gordon. With superior driving skills, good looks and a game show host stage presence, Gordon has it all," wrote Chris Jenkins in *USA Today*. [6]

"He changed what a Winston Cup driver is to a sponsor," said Ray Evernham, who won three championships as Gordon's crew chief before leaving to start his own team for Dodge. "Jeff is so good, speaking and with his television — Letterman and all that. He raised the bar for the rest of these young guys." [7]

Gordon was groomed to race at an early age. Born Aug. 4, 1971, he is the second child of Bill and Carol Gordon. His parents were divorced a year later, and his mother married Bickford, an auto-parts maker with a passion for racing.

Gordon said in an on-line interview that he started racing bicycles at age 6. Actually, he was about 4 ½ when his stepfather helped him onto a bike for a motocross race. His mother didn't like the inherent dangers of riding over large bumps amid groups of other boys. Bickford persisted and, by age 6, Gordon was competing in quarter-midget cars, a six-foot vehicle with a single-cylinder engine.

"It was fun for both of us," Bickford said. "I was living my childhood through him." Bickford was tough on the young prodigy. Gordon wasn't allowed to knock another driver aside en route to a victory. If he did make contact, his stepfather made him give up the trophy.

"The driving came pretty natural, but [Dad] never ever let me get overconfident," Gordon said. "He always made me work harder, work for more. He wanted me to be better."[8]

Gordon won his first of his two national quarter-midget championships at age 8 and raced year-round on weekends. At age 9, he climbed into a go-kart and started beating teenagers to the finish line. By the time he was 13, Gordon had moved up to Sprint cars. In 1986, Bickford decided there were more chances of success in Indiana, long a racing hotbed.[9] He relocated the family to tiny Pittsboro — still listed as Gordon's hometown, although he lives in North Carolina.*

Besides, Gordon only needed to be 14 to race on tracks there.

By then, Gordon was supporting the family with prize money. If money ran short, the family slept in a pick-up truck. Ironically, Bickford and Gordon no longer work together and rarely communicate. Gordon fired him in the mid-1990s.

"He's a father; he didn't want me to make any mistakes," said

---

* As with most everything under its control, NASCAR likes to orchestrate image. Drivers are listed by hometown regardless of where they actually live to give the illusion that the sport reaches all areas of this country. For many years, Gordon's California roots were ignored. Actually, most drivers live near their team headquarters in North Carolina. A handful, such as Mark Martin and Mike Skinner, reside in the Daytona Beach area. In the NASCAR records, however, Martin is living in Batesville, Arkansas, and Skinner in Susanville, California.

Gordon. "I wanted to learn. And, sometimes, you learn by making mistakes." [10]

In 1989, he joined open-wheel racing through USAC, which had once been the most important sanctioning body, but had been supplanted by NASCAR. In 1990, he won the USAC Midget title. A year later, Gordon stepped up to the USAC Silver Crown division and became the youngest driver to win that title.

His success naturally drew some interest from various NASCAR owners. He turned down an offer from Joe Gibbs — later better known as the coach of pro football's Washington Redskins — saying he was too young at that time. Instead, he participated in a driving school at North Carolina Speedway taught by old-time racer Buck Baker. A picture of the class shows a very youthful looking Gordon the end of the front line, almost out of place among the larger, older students.

"After my first day at the school, I knew where my future was," Gordon claimed in his autobiography. "I loved stock-car racing."

By then, Gordon had joined Rick Hendrick. The transition was not smooth. He was a Ford driver in the NASCAR Busch Series and driving for Bill Davis with Baby Ruth as a sponsor. But, he didn't have a Cup contract. Davis simply assumed that Gordon would be his driver in 1993 when the team began competing in the elite NASCAR Sprint Cup Series. [11]

His crew chief was Evernham, a former modified car driver from New Jersey, who had worked on Kulwicki championship team. The two clicked immediately.

In Atlanta during the fourth race of the new season, Hendrick watched Gordon smoothly cope with a mishandling car and reach Victory Lane. He assumed Gordon had a contract, but was told by Andy Graves, Gordon's roommate, that there wasn't one. [12]

Hendrick hesitated, not sure he wanted to be saddled with a

new driver and a new crew chief. "Ray was smart," Gordon explained. "He had driven a racecar before; I liked that. He understood me. We pretty much told Rick, 'Hey, Ray's a part of me.' " Hendrick finally agreed.

Then, it was the sponsor's turn.

"When he first laid eyes on Jeff Gordon, Lou Savelli wondered whether he had made a terrible mistake. The president of Du Pont's automotive-finishes division, Savelli had just staked about $11 million—and much of his aggressive growth strategy—on a stock car driven by the 20-year-old rookie. Stock-car racing was huge with Savelli's customers: automakers and repair-shop owners. So he saw the sponsorship as a way of putting them closer to the drivers they idolized. But, when Savelli met the young driver (in 1992), his heart sank. Slim and slight, he didn't have a Southern accent, and he was as polite as an altar boy. Could this guy really handle 700 horses at 200 mph against men much older, more experienced, and a whole lot ornerier? 'Was I wrong?' Savelli asked himself." [13]

No, was the answer.

"In 1991, the year before Savelli decided to sponsor Gordon, the automotive-refinishes group was a $500 million business. In 1999, revenues exceeded $1 billion. Savelli attributes 20 percent of the growth—$100 million—to his company's association with Gordon.

Savelli said his company earns $5 for every $1 he spends on the Gordon team, a return that'll bring a tear to any CFO's eye. "This has been magnificent for us, absolutely phenomenal," Savelli said. "He's helped us keep our current business and obtain new business. In three or four years, the deal paid for itself." [14]

Gordon has come out far ahead, too. He was the first race car driver with multi-million dollar endorsement deals. Companies that hired him by 1999 included Pepsi, Chesebrough-Pond's (Close

Up toothpaste), Edy's ice cream, Chevrolet, and Ray-Ban sunglasses. His success helped stock car racing camouflage its dingy origins.

"NASCAR has emerged with a very broad-based image on Madison Avenue that is far from the Southern cracker mentality that some people would have conceived for it recently," said David Falk, a prominent sports agent. [15]

"Can he do what Muhammed Ali and Jordan did and go beyond his sport?" asked Humpy Wheeler, president of Speedway Motorsports, once the nation's largest track operator. "He might, because he's the antithesis of what a racer should be. He's not a good ol' tobacco-chewing guy. But, he needs what Ali and Arnold Palmer had — great victories over tremendous competition. Now, he makes it look too easy." [16]

No one is complaining. With one race in 1992, Gordon gave his sport an entree into the youth market and Madison Avenue.

As a result, interest in stock car racing burgeoned. Everything Bill France envisioned was coming true. The bubble lasted until the first part of the 21st century. Jeff Gordon had given NASCAR another 10 years.

Attendance at NASCAR Sprint Cup events climbed 63 percent between 1990-1999, according to figures published in *Fortune* magazine. That's more than any other major sport. The NBA finished second, juiced by Michael Jordan's presence, and enjoyed a growth rate of 12 percent during that same time period. Gross retail sales of NASCAR-related apparel, die-cast cars, and other licensed products reached about $80 million in 1990 and crossed the $1 billion mark a decade later. Television ratings shot up, too, making NASCAR stock car racing the second-highest-rated sport on television behind pro football. [17]

Today, drivers are opting for NASCAR over open-wheel racing. That includes Danica Patrick, Sam Hornish Jr., A.J. Allmandinger,

Dario Franchitti and Juan Pablo Montoya. Few enjoyed any success: Hornish lost his ride at the end of 2015; Patrick lost her long-time sponsor at the same time. Franchitti fled back to Indy cars as did Montoya, who promptly won the 2015 Indianapolis 500. Montoya managed two NASCAR wins in eight years, one behind Robby Gordon who eked out three in more than 380 NASCAR starts for the best record among former open-wheel drivers. Neither Patrick nor Hornish have won a Sprint Cup race.

Jeff Gordon opened the door. When he arrived, only Dale Earnhardt was left from the type of roughnecks who started and built stock car racing. He and Gordon faced off virtually every weekend, generating even more interest in the sport. Earnhardt, burly and undignified, scarred and unvarnished, represented the old way; Gordon, squeaky clean and genteel, polite and smooth, illustrated where the sport was going.

Together, they helped stock car racing through another curve in the long road to acceptance and dominance.

CHAPTER 9: 2001
EARNHARDT'S DEATH

Jeff Gordon drove NASCAR into the upper levels of American sport, but the face of motorsports was Dale Earnhardt, a mustachioed Southerner with a mischievous smile that hid a fierce competitor. Known affectionately as the "Man in Black" and "The Intimidator," Earnhardt did not hesitate to knock drivers out of his way en route to 76 Winston Cup victories.

His almost playful manner also disguised a fierce businessman who forced NASCAR to pay him for any merchandise that bore his image or that of his car, the legendary No. 3 black Goodwrench Chevrolet.

He survived multiple crashes and dustups on the track until February 18, 2001. On the last lap of the Daytona 500, Earnhardt died after slamming into a wall.

That incredible, awful and dramatic event stunned race fans, leaders of stock car racing and the nation. His death also almost eviscerated the sport. It was one turn that no one in the sport expected.

Earnhardt was more than a single competitor, not just one of 43 drivers who lined up every Sunday and steered their high-powered cars across the start/finish line and headed for the checkered flag hundreds of miles away. He was stock car racing.

"Richard Petty may have created NASCAR, but it was Dale Earnhardt who drove it off television sets and into living rooms across the nation. He was the one who took the image of greasy good ol' boys and reshaped it into clean young marketed men. And he did it all by himself, with NASCAR happy to ride right along on his back bumper. The sport sold the Man in Black, it sold No. 3 decals, it sold Chevrolets.

Earnhardt collected millions of dollars from the sport, but the sport earned even more from him. It earned a spot in mainstream America and on Wall Street." [1]

"According to a Harris Interactive Poll, 90 percent of the general population recognized Earnhardt's name in a January 2000 survey, just 9 percent less than recognized (Michael) Jordan. Earnhardt's archrival, Jeff Gordon, was recognized by 72 percent of those polled. Further quantifying Earnhardt's importance to the sport was that 35 percent of people who attended a NASCAR event in the past twelve months cited Earnhardt as their favorite driver," ESPN reported in 2001. [2]

The report continued, "And when sports fans were asked by Harris Interactive who their favorite sports team or race driver was, Earnhardt placed third — just behind the New York Yankees and Dallas Cowboys."

His death, ESPN said, "calls off all projections — at least at this point — that seek to declare NASCAR as the fifth major sport in the near future."

The impact of his death, one pundit wrote, was like Michael Jordon dropping dead in the middle of a basketball game. He was the smiling face and intense eyes of a sport that had projected only a dour, surly image before. He meant more than Tiger Woods meant to golf in his heyday. Woods didn't play every tournament; Dale Earnhardt did not miss a race. He was always there, racing with broken bones, racing as if that was all there was to life, and taking millions of spectators along with him for the ride.

"NASCAR's merchandise sales hit $2 billion in the last year (2003), and, in large part, the sport has Dale Earnhardt Sr. to thank for that. Earnhardt is credited with having elevated racing from cult status to nationwide craze," wrote Penelope Patsuris in the 2004 *Forbes* magazine. [3]

Now, he was dead, killed in a seemingly innocuous mishap. People simply expected him to walk away, the way he had in 1997 after a crash in the Daytona 500. He had flipped his car upside down on the backstretch, crushing its roof. Then, while climbing into the track ambulance, Earnhardt noticed his No. 3 Goodwrench Chevrolet had rolled upright.

"I got in the ambulance," he told reporters later, "and when I looked back and saw the wheels were still on that thing, I told the guy in there, 'Hey, see if it cranks.' It cranked, so I said, 'Give me my car back.' "

Seconds later, he was driving it into the pits while trying to see through a narrow slit that remained of his shattered windshield.

Fans loved him for it.

Now, the question was: would they remain with the sport if Earnhardt were gone?

No one knew.

"What does the sport do without him? Where does his sport go without him? Who will replace him?" Dave Van Dyck of FOX Sports asked. [4]

In Manchester England, the famed *Guardian* noted, "It's not clear where NASCAR will go from here. Earnhardt was the fourth NASCAR driver to die in a year. A record like that in any other sport would invite commissions of inquiry and calls for a reform and even abolution." [5]

Drivers were not sure they wanted to go on to the next race, at North Carolina Speedway. Earnhardt's son and namesake had to hold a news conference with the car's owner, Richard Childress, to say that Earnhardt would have wanted them to continue.

"We're gonna do what Dale would want us to do, and that's race," a saddened Childress said.

Earnhardt definitely would have.

Born in Kannapolis, North Carolina, Ralph Dale Earnhardt was the son of a Hall of Fame driver Ralph Earnhardt. A photo of his father, taken in the 1940s as he sat in the front seat of his car, shows a pleasant young man looking intimidated by his surroundings and yet courageously planning to continue. His son inherited that same fortitude.

Dale — he never went by his first name — left school after eighth grade and eventually became a service station attendant and mechanic. By age 18, he had a wife and a child to support. As a result, to race, he would scavenge parts from junkyards and the station to build cars able to withstand the rigors of the track.

When his father died in 1973 while working on a car, Earnhardt focused on his racing career. He always said he was trying to match his father and build on the family legacy. That was in keeping with the tradition of motor sports, which has always been a family sport. Few of today's drivers completed the hard journey to the top series in NASACR without following in a relative's tire tracks.

Earnhardt made his debut in NASCAR elite series in 1975. He was brash, prone to accidents and more likely to end up on the sidelines than finish a race. Still, in 1979, his first full year, Earnhardt won the Rookie of the Year Award.*

---

*   NASCAR has arcane rules for rookies. As long as a driver does not compete in more than seven races in a single year, he is qualified for the rookie award the year he tops that mark. As a result, "rookies" may actually have a lot of experience before being considered for the coveted prize. Moreover, a driver must declare he is aiming at the award to be considered for it.

A year later, Earnhardt became the only driver to win the championship the year after taking home the rookie trophy. He linked up with Richard Childress Racing in 1981, joining the one-time driver to create one of the most famous and successful partnerships in any sport.

In the late 1990s, Earnhardt formed his own team, although continuing to race for Childress. Only NASCAR allows team owners to drive for one team while fielding their own entries. That's like George Steinbrenner owning the New York Yankees and playing for the Boston Red Sox.

In 2001, Earnhardt went into the final lap of the 43rd Daytona 500 in third place. He was following cars owned by his own team, Dale Earnhardt Enterprises, even though he drove for Richard Childress. Michael Waltrip, whom Earnhardt hired late in 2000, was in first place. That was unexpected. Waltrip, brother of retired NASCAR champion Darrell Waltrip, had not won in a record 465 straight races, and Earnhardt had been roundly criticized for adding him to the elite DEI team. In second was Dale Earnhardt Jr., who had never won the Daytona 500 and had been erratic on the track in his rookie season the year before.

Although no one knows for sure what was in his mind, Earnhardt appeared to be blocking other competitors from gaining on the lead two cars. Purists insist he was racing for a win even though his hand-picked driver was in first and his son in second.

Regardless, his car was nudged by a car behind him, then turned by another car. The second accident sent the No. 3 directly into the wall at nearly 200 mph. NASCAR later said the impact broke Earnhardt's safety belt and caused his head to snap back violently. He died instantly, becoming the first — and, to date, only — driver to be fatally injured during the Daytona 500 in its history.

At that point, NASCAR seemed fatally wounded, too. Earnhardt's death added to what was becoming an intolerable toll, particularly since NASCAR had seemingly delayed the addition of "softer" walls invented and used by its counterpart, the Indy Racing League. In May 2000, NASCAR Busch Series driver Adam Petty, the grandson of stock car great Richard Petty, was killed in a crash during practice at Loudon, New Hampshire. Two months later, NASCAR Winston Cup driver Kenny Irwin was killed in a similar accident at New Hampshire International Speedway in almost the identical spot on the track. Then, NASCAR Craftsman Truck Series driver Tony Roper was killed in October at Texas Motor Speedway.

Now, Earnhardt.

Crashes supposedly helped rivet attention to the track. Deaths, however, deflated enthusiasm. No one knew how fans would react at the next 2001 race, which was scheduled for at North Carolina Speedway in Rockingham, NC. The race there was usually not well attended anyway. (In fact, ISC Corporation, which, like NASCAR, was also founded by Bill France and owns tracks around the country, sold the track in 2004, and it was quickly shuttered for a few years.) While makeshift memorials to Earnhardt piled up, including one by the massive rock outside North Carolina Speedway, tickets sales remained slow. ISC counts fannies in the seats, not pedals on roses strewn by the track.

The 2001 race was held, of course. The season would continue, even if the pilot had left the engine room. However, without something dramatic, it was an open question how long NASCAR could endure. Two things took place that weekend to help change that gloomy perspective.

First, Earnhardt Jr. rolled into tiny Rockingham to race. "He has been everybody's strength," said then-DEI teammate Kenny Wallace. "That strength helped a lot of people get through Dale's death… (At Rockingham), we all showed up and it's like — 'Man, we got to race this weekend?' And, then Dale Jr. showed up, and it was OK. His presence made everybody feel better."

Then, Steve Park, another DEI teammate somehow won the race. It was an unlikely victory. Park had only one other victory with DEI — and would be fired in 2004 — but showed great tenacity by returning to racing after a rehabilitating injury in 1998 almost ended his career.

The Associated Press report that day clearly indicated what the media thought about the win.

"Steve Park drove his Dale Earnhardt Inc.-owned No. 1 Pennzoil Chevrolet to the stripe first in what may become known as the most popular win of the 2001 Winston Cup season."

The drivers also knew what the win meant. "Congratulations to those guys," said second-place finished Bobby Labonte. "It was a great run for them. They needed that."

The team understood that the fans needed it, too.

"Almost immediately after securing the victory, Park shoved a No. 3 Earnhardt flag out his window. Waving the hat in celebration and tribute to his car owner, Park started a 'Polish Victory Lap' by reversing direction around the track. Teammate Michael Waltrip stopped along side Park and the two exchanged a high-five while Earnhardt banners, flags, and hats waved delightedly from the crowd.

"It's been a tough week and this is a dream finish," Park said. "Dale's gone, but he's not forgotten, and he's going to be with all the DEI drivers the rest of the year."[6]

"With his win at 'The Rock,' Steve Park made the first move in what would be a long healing process," the DEI website noted.

" … to go out there and win in his honor without a doubt has lifted everyone's spirits," Park said. "It's just part of the healing process that we're all going to have to go through."

"Everyone involved with NASCAR got permission to feel good again Monday, on a sun-drenched day at North Carolina Speedway that eventually rose to the level of fine drama," Scott Fowler wrote in the *Charlotte Observer*. "It wasn't a normal race day, of course. An emotional cauldron still brews in NASCAR, full of safety concerns and questions about how to replace the sport's Michael Jordan and a terrible sadness for Earnhardt and his family. Yet the mood felt lighter Monday."[7]

It got even better less than a month later. NASCAR has often been accused of scripting races, akin to professional wrestling. No one in the sport would have had the imagination to come up with this scenario.

After Earnhardt's death, Childress plucked an unknown driver in NASCAR's second tier — the Busch Series — to take over the vacant seat. Kevin Harvick was already committed to his Busch Series team, so decided to race full time in both series. Many drivers regularly compete in more than one race during a weekend when both top touring series have events on the same weekend and the same track. For example, Mark Martin, a long-time competitor in the top NASCAR Series, had won more races (49) than anyone since the Busch Series was formed in 1982 before Kyle Busch surpassed him. Harvick proposed racing two races every weekend, regardless of the locale. Childress agreed.

Harvick declined to appear in the No. 3 car made famous by Earnhardt, so Childress repainted it with white colors and renumbered it as 29. Everyone knew it was Earnhardt's car. The No. 3 didn't return until Childress' grandson, Austin Dillon, raced it in 2014 NASCAR Sprint Cup Series, although the number was used on a Dillon car in the NASCAR Xfinity series starting in 2012.

Then, at Atlanta Motor Speedway in the fourth race of the 2001 season, Harvick unexpectedly and inexplicably held the lead on the last lap, charging down the backstretch toward the checkered flag with Jeff Gordon beside him. The image was brought back memories of Earnhardt-Gordon duels that had helped transform NASCAR.

Gordon was more than the driver with the most wins of any active competitor and the man who had banked more money than any NASCAR driver in history, he was the counterpart to Earnhardt's hard, rough-hewn visage. As noted earlier, Gordon had come from California, been a winner even as a child, and still looks far younger than his years. Clean faced, almost cherubic, he was a far cry from the tough, sandpapered moonshiners who emerged from the bag woods, spit tobacco and loved to run someone off the road while swilling rotgut at 150 mph. He was a choir boy — an image he retains despite a messy divorce in 2003 — who was so much Earnhardt's opposite, that he attracted hate in equal percentages to the affection afforded Earnhardt.

This writer attended a free movie during Speedweeks 2000 in which fans booed and threw things every time Gordon's familiar No. 24 DuPont Chevrolet appeared on the screen. Even in 2004, during a showing of a movie in Daytona USA, fans there hissed and yelled whenever Gordon's car popped into view. Since Gordon won four titles between 1992 and 2001, thwarting Earnhardt's hopes of capturing a record eighth championship, his position as the chief NASCAR villain was completely entrenched.

There he was, straining to pass Earnhardt's old car on the final lap of a race.

"I can't really recall the last few laps of the race," Harvick said later. "I had to go home and watch the tape to figure out what was going on. It was pretty crazy out there the last five or six laps. But, you really couldn't write a script any better than the way things happened."[8]

Harvick somehow won by .06 seconds.

"I don't even know how to put this into words, to tell the honest to God's truth," Harvick said. "It took an extra lap afterwards to get the emotional part out of the way, then pulling into Victory Lane and seeing all those guys who have put their arms out and supported me through probably one of the hardest times of their lives and the hardest situation of my life … "

Like the fans, Harvick knew who deserved the credit.

"I think Dale Earnhardt was in the passenger seat of this car today," he said. "Somebody was making me go a lot better than I was." Added owner Childress, who was in tears after the race, "I just kept praying for Dale to help us out. He gave us the help we needed. I know he's somewhere. I can see him with that mustache of his just breaking into a big grin."

Everything about the win evoked Earnhardt's memory. "The finish was eerily similar to the spring race last year, when Earnhardt beat Bobby Labonte by .010 seconds for his record ninth victory on Atlanta's 1.5-mile oval. And the scene afterward was similar to that when Earnhardt won the 1998 Daytona 500 and crew members from every team lined up along pit road to congratulate him. As Harvick made his victory lap, waving three fingers out the window to symbolize Earnhardt's No. 3, the other crews gathered to greet him as he came off the track."9

"The GM Goodwrench car circling in a Polish victory lap with Harvick holding three fingers out the window again brought back a rush emotion. This was a healing moment for NASCAR. We remembered the legend and honored the future in the same moment." [10]

The sport made the final step back from the brink in July 2001. Nothing could have been more emotional that the return of the elite series to the track where its greatest driver died. The Pepsi 400, run under the lights at Daytona International Speedway, drew the attention of media from around the world. Ratings after the race were dynamite. According to published reports, about 25 million people tuned in for the Pepsi 400, making it the most-watched NASCAR race in prime time. The first race aired by NBC under its new $2.8 billion contract with NASCAR recorded a 6.1 national rating, which was 17 percent higher than the 2000 Pepsi 400.

Earnhardt Jr., who had endured a tough season on and off the track, led most of the night, but with nine laps to go, a caution slowed the action after Gordon's car started to emit smoke. The drivers lined up for one last run for Victory Lane. For any driver, a win at Daytona — in the summer or during the Daytona 500 — would be a highlight of a career. In some cases, like unknown Derrike Cope, who won the Daytona 500 in 1990, it actually made a career.

Earnhardt took the green flag in seventh, behind Waltrip, Johnny Benson, Tony Stewart and Bobby Labonte and two others.

When the green flag waved, Earnhardt Jr. simply blew by everyone on the track in a magical spurt that brought fans to their feet in a sustained ovation.

Teammate Michael Waltrip tucked in behind Earnhardt Jr.'s No. 8 Budweiser Chevrolet and helped shove him across the finish line.

Waltrip made no move to attempt to pass.

"I just told him this was what it's all about," Waltrip said. "He called me the Monday after the Daytona 500. Of course, we were all grieving. He just said, 'I was committed to you, buddy.' Those words kept going through my mind."

It was almost unanimous in the garage after the race: If it couldn't have been them, Junior was the one they wanted to see win.

"It's hard to imagine anybody you would want to win here any more than Little Earnhardt," driver Jeff Burton said. "It's good to see. This sport lost a hero. A lot of people lost a hero, but he lost a hero and his dad."

Earnhardt Jr. understood what the race signified. In the post-race media conference, he said, "This means a lot to a lot of people. I'm having a good time with it; it makes me feel good. And, I think a lot more people really needed this probably more than I did."

One author wrote, "NASCAR was in mourning, perhaps even shock, nearly five months after the loss of its 'Intimidator.' But, when Junior took the checkered flag a few hundred yards from where his father perished in turn 4, sorrow turned to joy. For many, the healing process began that night, with the sight of Junior and teammate Michael Waltrip embracing on the roof of the No. 8 Chevrolet." [10]

Fans were equally emotional. The victories proved that Dale Earnhardt, in some inexplicable way, lived on through his cars. He was still the embodiment of stock car racing. Park, Harvick and Earnhardt Jr. each claimed that The Intimidator sat in the passenger seat. His presence guaranteed that fans would not leave. They had been reassured. The road had curved dramatically, but their leader — and the leader of the entire sport — was still at the helm.

CHAPTER 10: 2004
EARNHARDT JR.'S SUCCESSOR

For three years after the death of Dale Earnhardt, stock car racing fans waited for someone to step into the void creating by the passing of the driver known as The Intimidator.

His chief rival, Jeff Gordon, was not the man to take the sport on his shoulders. He was still the altar boy amid ruffians. His divorce from a former Miss Winston helped properly tarnish his goody-goody image, but did not endear him to the conservative, family-first NASCAR crowd.

Kevin Harvick, the youngster who took Earnhardt's open seat, seemed to have the inside track. He won the 2001 NASCAR Busch Series title and the Rookie of the Year award in the NASCAR Winston Cup Series in the same year. He manfully competed in all but one race in both series, an unheard of accomplishment. His dual success made the effort even more remarkable. The Californian married a former race publicist mid-way through that incredible season, adding another plus for an eager audience. Unfortunately, his success waned in 2002 and 2003; and Harvick failed to finish in the top 10 in 2004. It would be another decade before he would match his early success. After three years in Earnhardt's old car, he was just another driver in a bland field.

Kurt Busch tried the nasty route without Earnhardt's charisma.

Then, he destroyed his credibility in late 2003 by saying Jimmy Spencer had deliberately provoked him. Busch slugged Spencer, only to be shamed when taped recordings of his in-car conversation indicated that he had done far more than Spencer to initiate the fight. His brother, Kyle, who has been an impressive winner in all three top series, has generated a darker image without a corresponding surge in popularity.

Tony Stewart drew attention with his bad-boy routine, which included a near-mugging of a photographer and a fan as well as on-track incidents. He won three championships, a requisite for fan adoration. Nevertheless, Stewart failed to achieve great popularity, the result of a surly public personality combined with limited interest in media self promotion. He eventually ran over a fellow driver on the track and left the series in 2015 for a while. His retirement in 2016 generated little more than a yawn.

No one else really stood out. Jimmie Johnson eventually won five straight championships, and later added two more, but never built a national following. He has been criticized for a lack of a personality. So has Matt Kenseth, the 2003 champion. A television commercial played off his image by projecting him as a robot. Mark Martin, 45 in 2004, continually challenged for the title, but was too old for the young crowd and announced he was reducing his schedule in 2005 in a prelude to retirement.

Long-time heroes, like Rusty Wallace, Dale Jarrett, Terry Labonte and Bill Elliott, were rarely competitive, planned to retire or reduced their participation to a part-time basis. Younger, would-be stars, like Bobby Labonte and Jeff Burton, fell back into the pack after some early success and remain essentially anonymous. Ward Burton, Jeff's older brother, may have won the 2002 Daytona 500, but that was a fluke — the two drivers in front late in the race ended up colliding. He also has few fans. With a couple of years, he was out of the sport and reportedly living in the Virginia woods.

Sales of the 2003 Daytona 500 official souvenir program with Burton's car prominently displayed on it attracted little attention compared with a generic cover. ISC traditionally produced covers that featured last year's winner. There was so little interest in Burton that six different covers were produced. The ones featuring Burton was later sent to the dump. Today, given their rarity, they are probably more valuable than any of the others.

Also-rans like Joe Nemechek, Spencer and Greg Biffle have no chance. By 2017, all three had lost rides. Younger drivers — including Brendan Gaughan, Kasey Kahne and Scott Wimmer — that never achieved much success. Gaughan never get a chance; he was fired after the 2004 season and may end up on the sidelines with Roy "Buckshot" Jones, another young hotshot who had one year to succeed and failed. Wimmer got a headstart by garnering a drunk driving conviction, but then dissipated any possible fan enthusiasm by apologizing. He was no longer in the top series soon after.

Who was left to replace Earnhardt?

That is not an idle question. When Michael Jordan retired, interest in professional basketball fell precipitously. The National Basketball Association has continually tried to find a replacement. Kobe Bryant stepped into the gap along with Shaquille O'Neal. LeBron James of the Cleveland Cavaliers has followed with Seth Curry seemingly next in line. Nevertheless, the NBA still hasn't recovered from Jordan's retirement.

Baseball rode Mark McGwire and Sammy Sosa's homerun battle in 1998 to recover affection lost by a strike and then touted Barry Bonds homerun-record run in 2003. Since then, the game has been tarnished by a drug scandal, and no one player has emerged to carry the sport as Mickey Mantle, Snyder and Willie Mays did in the 1950s. As a result, the New York Yankees served as everyone's devil (except for New Yorkers, of course), but the Bronx Bombers have drifted back into the back. From 2002, the Arizona Diamondbacks, the Florida Marlins and the Boston Red Sox have taken turns slaying the dragon, helping boost interest and attendance. David vs. Goliath is a good show in any era. Still, the greatest of the superstars currently competing, Mike Trout, remains almost anonymous on a bad Angels team.

Hockey survived a strike and then sold television rights to the Outdoor Network, which was viewed by only a tiny percentage of Americans. That was not a recipe for success. Today, hockey games appear on NBC, but viewership is small compared with other major sports.

Soccer has limped along for years. David Beckham was brought in prior to the 2007 season in hopes of boosting interest, but most Americans in a poll had no idea who the English star was. The women on the national team have garnered far more attention that any team in Major League Soccer, but that didn't translate into a success league. Soccer still attracts more support worldwide than any sport, but has languished in this country.

Only football has endured without always having one person for fans to concentrate on.

Racing, like all American sports, needs a centerpiece, a driver like Earnhardt who serves as a magnet for both fans and sponsors. After all, without someone to focus on, the sport quickly deteriorates into the reality that souped-up cars are simply but rapidly going around in circles. Even the touted Car of Tomorrow, which NASCAR introduced to the Sprint Cup series in 2008, offered little excuse for casual fans to pay hefty ticket prices.

Stock car moguls only had to look at their counterparts in the Indy car realm to see what could happen without a central star. In the mid-1990s, that sport split into two rival series — Indy Racing League (IRL) and Championship Auto Racing Teams

(CART). The IRL built its season around the Indianapolis 500, but fields few stars and attracted little interest beyond the historic race. A series of unknowns won anyway, while breathless announcers tried to make it sound as if Kenny Brack, Juan Pablo Montoya (who soon head off to NASCAR only to return after limited success there) and Eddie Cheever were in the league with icons like A.J. Foyt, Al Unser or Bobby Rahal.

One star, Sam Hornish Jr., promptly was hired by NASCAR as was Danica Patrick. Both won races in the Indy circuit, but have accomplished little in NASCAR.

CART didn't have the Indianapolis 500, but featured the drivers like Michael Andretti and Al Unser Jr. But, they were at the ends of their careers. No names, no great races. CART finally folded its tent in 2003 and reemerged in 2004 as, basically, a minor league. The IRL soldiers on, but now attracts far fewer fans than in the heyday of open-wheel racing. Its biggest event is still the Indianapolis 500, but the owners of the series reportedly make far more money letting stock cars and their fans into the Indianapolis Motor Speedway for the Brickyard 400 than they do for any of their series' own races.

The decline of interest in Indy cars has left the focus on stock cars, but the sport definitely needed a new star to take advantage of the opportunity. Richard Petty was the lodestone from the 1960s through the early 1990s. Earnhardt followed him.

Next up: another Earnhardt.

That has not been a surprise. From the first, Dale Earnhardt Jr. was expected to succeed his father in the affection of fans and as the workhorse of the sport. He simply needed time to get into position.

Born October 10, 1974, seven and a half years before his dad's Winston Cup debut, young Dale endured an emotionally tough childhood. His parents divorced when he was three; his father, who admittedly exuded little affection or warmth, concentrated on winning car races and sent his son to military school.

Money was not in short supply after Earnhardt's career started rolling. The Man in Black earned $26.5 million in 1999. Dale Jr. reportedly sold $30 million worth of souvenirs before he ever drove in a NASCAR Winston Cup race.

At age 17, the younger Earnhardt got into his first race car. He competed on the small tracks in the Carolinas, but posted only three wins in his first 100 starts. In 1996, Dale Earnhardt hired his son to drive in the NASCAR Busch Series. Maybe he saw something in the lanky youngster. His other son, Kerry, raced for years, but was been unable to emerge from his father's massive shadow. He retired in 2009, never having won a race in any of the NASCAR series.

"Whenever Dad got killed at Daytona, it all came crumbling down," Earnhardt said in 2016. "He was my supporter, and I didn't have anyone else backing me with that career. They decided not to pursue that, so we just threw it out the window."

Kerry's son, Jeffrey, 26, began his full-time NASCAR Sprint Cup career in 2016. So far, he has shown none of the charisma of his grandfather or uncle.

Dale Earnhardt Jr. has been the one to carry on the family race legacy. Earnhardt Jr. does have some of his father's traits. He described them in a 2001 *Playboy* magazine interview, which in itself gives a hint of his popularity. After all, in 2000, he had ended up 16th in the final standings with two wins. But, he was an Earnhardt.

"Some of it's reaction time and peripheral vision. People say that my dad had eyes in the back of his head, and I'm good that way, too," Earnhardt Jr. said. "My pulse rate's slower than average, like his was. But, there's confidence, too. Just being around him, seeing him win all those races, gives me an edge over a guy whose father wasn't a driver. I'll go up against that guy, thinking I'm going to beat him because it's in my blood. Even if I didn't inherit my father's ability, that helps." [1]

Actually, he had already flashed his talent. "Little E" — one of his two familiar nicknames; the other, inevitably, is "Junior" — won back-to-back NASCAR Busch Series titles in 1998-1999 and joined the senior circuit as NASCAR's most heralded newcomer since Jeff Gordon in 1992.

But, unlike his father, he didn't win the rookie title that year (Kenseth did), and then showed only glimpses of his ability in the next two years. Fans lapped up his No. 8 Budweiser souvenirs, but Earnhardt Jr. seemingly was turning out more like Kyle Petty, Richard's son, who had quickly fell back in the pack and stayed there throughout his career. He garnered eight wins in 26 years and only one since 1994 before retiring in 2008. Charismatic and handsome, Kyle was supposed to be the new NASCAR savior when he stated racing in 1979, but now is better known for his laudable charity efforts than by anything on the track.

The fear was that Earnhardt Jr. would fall into the same pattern.

That changed in 2004. One race introduced Dale Jr. as a worthy success to his father.

Earnhardt had needed a record 20 starts before winning his first Daytona 500. Once, a pigeon hit his car and ruined the dynamics. Another time, a last-lap flat tire deflated his hopes. Hard luck dogged him until 1998, when a late-race caution allowed him to roll unchallenged across the start/finish line to the thunderous roar of the more than 200,000 fans and the open applause of his rivals. The win created one of racing's most cherished scenes: the black No. 3 Chevrolet rolling down pit road while every rival crewmember lined up to congratulate Earnhardt before he pulled into Victory Lane.

Junior didn't wait two decades. He won the 2004 Daytona 500 in his fifth try, a victory made more significant because of the situation.

First, the elite series had a new sponsor for the first time in 33 years. RJR had stepped aside midway through a five-year contract, beset by rising legal fees as states and individuals began suing for damages linked to cigarette smoke. In addition, more government-mandated rules limited where and how tobacco companies could promote their products. Hamstrung, RJR and NASCAR agreed that stock car racing might be better off with a new sponsor. Moreover, NASCAR wanted to cut its ties to an unsavory product, even though its stands are filled with a high percentage of smokers.

After NASCAR opened the bidding to rename its top series, Nextel, the fifth-ranked telecommunications company in size in 2003, agreed to pay a record $70 million a year for a decade for the privilege of replacing Winston. No other naming agreement in sports carried such a hefty price tag. It was a gamble for Nextel, since NASCAR fans are not considered technologically sophisticated, but the opportunity for publicity and name identification outweighed any potential shortfalls, company officials said. The company merged with Sprint late in 2004, which replaced Nextel with its own name.

The 2004 Daytona 500 was the NASCAR Nextel Cup Series' first race.

Second, President George W. Bush decided at the last minute to take actor Ben Affleck's place as grand marshal. Affleck was relegated to riding around in the pace car, although he had been touted as grand marshal in the official souvenir program.

Bush, facing a tough battle for re-election, played the NASCAR card throughout his 2004 campaign. He was only the second sitting president to attend a NASCAR race and the first to take in the Daytona 500 in person. Prior to the race, Air Force One circled low over the Speedway to give racing fans a close look at a symbol of the presidency. Then, Bush stuck around for two hours, but left midway through the race.

He might have been overshadowed by Earnhardt Jr.'s victory anyway.

"Considering the dynamics of Sunday's affair — with the president on hand, the overwhelming aura of change throughout the sport and, maybe above all else, the eerie feeling that Big E was in the house — we'll look back at Feb. 15, 2004 five years from now as a seminal day in the evolution of a juggernaut.... I personally think Sunday's race was huge. The competition may have been ho-hum, but NASCAR will gain fans from it. Junior's victory instantly gives Nextel's decision legitimacy. You'll read about it in *People* magazine and see highlights on Access Hollywood and (ESPN) Sports Center," wrote Marty Smith of Turner Sports Interactive. [2]

The win was more impressive considering how Earnhardt Jr. pulled it off. He made a startling, unaided charge past Stewart with about 18 laps to go. To pass another car at Daytona, which requires restrictor plates on car engines to slow them down, drivers invariably need someone to push them. Earnhardt Jr. had no assistance. He didn't need it.

"I can't believe I passed him by myself," Earnhardt Jr. said. "I don't know what was going on. It was like a magic trick."

As CNN noted, "This one proved he's definitely his father's son. At the end of lap 180, Earnhardt Jr. dipped to the inside without any drafting help and came within a foot of Stewart's car at nearly 190 mph through the trioval. Then. Junior went right on by."

"I think his father's really proud today," said Stewart, who made three futile efforts to pass Earnhardt Jr. prior to the checkered flag. "If I could have held him off, had him finish second, I would have done it in a heartbeat. But, there was no holding that kid back today." [3]

As CBS News noted, "NASCAR could hardly have asked for more." [4]

Once the checkered flag waved, the huge crowd exploded in celebration. Earnhardt Jr. drove around to the start/finish line, got out of his car and saluted the fans.

"I just wanted to shout at the fans, wave at them, hear what they had to say," Earnhardt Jr. said.

"And there were plenty of them. He has so many fans, in fact, they've been dubbed by some as Earnhardt's Army," wrote Mike Harris of the Associated Press. [5]

"When I walk around with Junior, I feel like I'm with Elvis," said Martin Truex Jr., whom Earnhardt hired to drive the Busch Series car he co-owns with stepmother Teresa Earnhardt. [6]

After the race, Earnhardt Jr. "pumped his fist and jumped into the arms of his crew, who lifted him on their shoulders for all to see. Then he climbed back into the No. 8 Chevrolet and attempted a few doughnuts in the grass — just like his father after the 1998 race." [7]

The victory came six years to the day that his father won his only Daytona 500.

It also cemented Earnhardt Jr.'s position as the leader of stock car racing and guaranteed that the sport will endure for as few more years, even though its frontrunner is almost abashed by the role.

"It's overwhelming," Earnhardt Jr. said. "It's kind of an embarrassing form of flattery, if you will, to be considered (the pioneer changing the face of the sport)."

"When I was 18 years old, that definitely wasn't what I was aiming for. I didn't even have the vision or foresight to see that and target that. But things have fallen into place one after another. Circumstances have evolved and here we are." [8]

"It's overwhelming to have the kind of popularity that he has," said Ty Norris, executive vice president of Dale Earnhardt Inc., which fielded Earnhardt's No. 8 Chevrolet. He shifted to the No. 88 in 2008. "He constantly sits there and asks, 'Why? Why all of a sudden am I important? Because I wasn't important before and I'm not any different. I just drive race cars.' It bothers him because he thinks it's superficial. He almost feels like it's not deserved, but he can't change what's been thrust upon him. All he can do is deal with it." [9]

As a reporter noted, "In the garage area onlookers crowd around Junior's car and hauler to watch. Fans turn out in droves at his public appearances. He recently was on the cover of *Sports Illustrated*, tabbed as the man who will drive NASCAR's future." [10]

Ironically, Dale Earnhardt Jr. doesn't like the attention.

"I feel so undeserving sometimes because we run like crap on the race track and we still get all this attention, being the focal point of the sport and we're going to lead the sport into the new millennium, whatever," he said recently. "We go to all these appearances and all these people show up, and I never get used to it. It's good, it's fun, the excitement is great, but it makes me a little nervous sometimes, because I never get used to it. I wonder whether I ever will." [11]

He will have to do. Stock car racing, like all sports, needs a dominant personality, someone the sport can promote, someone the fans can live vicariously through.

Golf had Tiger Woods and now Jordon Spieth. Baseball had Mickey Mantle. Basketball has LeBron James and an onrushing Seth Curry. Stock car racing has Dale Earnhardt Jr., who has won the fan poll since 2003 to determine the most popular driver in the sport.

One race in 2004 guaranteed his lofty position and ensured that NASCAR has a new hero to bank on.

CHAPTER 11:
FUTURE

Having careened around one tricky corner into another, can stock car racing continue to thrive without colliding with a wall?

Maybe. On the surface, the sport looks to be in very good shape. The number of television viewers has fallen off a little from the peak, but stock car racing has clearly moved beyond its southern roots with tracks scattered around the country. Its drivers are given equal status with other significant athletes; races are accorded the same coverage as other major events.

The average NASCAR fan, according to NASCAR-supplied demographics, earns $68,267, hardly the income of a backwoods yokel. Besides, 60 percent have a college education.

The sport is also drawing young people, the prime target of advertisers: 11 percent of NASCAR fans are age 18-24; 21 percent are 25-34; 26 percent are 35-44; 19 percent are 45-54; 15 percent are 55-64; and 9 percent are 65 or older.

The majority is male, but 41 percent are female. The growth of support among women continues the gradual trend in the statistic and reflects the widening influence of the sport.

Stock car racing is also making inroads among minorities. A recent NASCAR report claims 24.5 percent of its fans are African-

American.[1]

As a result of such impressive statistics, a lot of big companies have climbed the fence and jumped into the stock car arena. They are enchanted by the loyalty fans show to businesses that back racing. According to published reports, the Olympics' loyalty rate is 28 percent, while the NFL is 36 percent. The NBA and Major League Baseball are both measured at 38 percent. Golf's is 47 percent. In contrast, NASCAR's loyalty rate tops 72 percent.

That doesn't mean there aren't concerns about the future of the sport. Stock car racing faces some severe problems that will have to be addressed to keep it on track.

Race Relations

Despite the widening minority fan base, NASCAR remains the last racial holdout in sports. Few drivers are black, even though NASCAR annually insists it's trying to recruit more minority drivers. To date, there have been only four: Wendell Scott, who is the only black driver to win a Winston Cup Series race; Willy T. Ribbs, who raced three times in the Winston Cup series in 1986; and Bill Lester.

Lester, who once complained he could not get his license to compete, was the only black driver in any of the top three NASCAR series in recent years. At 40, much older than a typical rookie, he got one Xfinity Series start in 1999 and moved full time into the truck series in 2002. These days, after only a few Sprint Cup starts, he's racing in the Rolex Grand Am Series, far away from the limelight enjoyed by his Sprint Cup counterparts.

Darrell "Bubba" Wallace Jr. is the only black driver today competing in any of NASCAR's top series. He drives in the Xfinity Series.

As a sign of how desperate the situation is, Hendrick Motorsports in 2004 signed a bi-racial high school freshman from

Kansas, named Chase Austin. He couldn't even drive in any of the top series for three years. He couldn't even drive to the grocery store then.

Austin's mother, Marianne, made light of the debate over her son's age.

"Pretty soon, we'll see kids in diapers and it'll be, 'He waddles well. Let's get him,'" she told the Associated Press.

Austin is listed as having raced in an Indy car for the last time in 2012, long after being dropped from stock car racing ranks.

For NASCAR, however, any driver with some African genes in him is a start in the right direction. Since its founding in 1948, only one black driver, Wendell Scott — who often had to pass as white — has won a NASCAR race, and that was back in 1963. Officials reportedly named another driver the winner to avoid having to give Scott the trophy in front of fans in Jacksonville, Florida.

NASCAR officials said a scoring error was responsible for allowing another driver to accept the winner's trophy. Scott doubted that explanation. "Everybody in the place knew I had won the race," he said years later, "but the promoters and NASCAR officials didn't want me out there kissing any beauty queens or accepting any awards." [2]

NASCAR also hasn't done itself any favors when trying to reach out to the black community. In 2003, NASCAR received tremendous negative publicity after newspapers revealed that the company privately funneled money to Rev. Jesse Jackson's Rainbow/PUSH Coalition. According to published accounts, NASCAR paid an affiliate of the group a total of $250,000, but ended funding in 2003 after the criticism started. In typical NASCAR manner, the sanctioning body did not announce the initial donation or tell Jackson of the cutoff.

Charles Farrell, a spokesman for Rainbow's sports division

said at the time, "We have had no contact whatsoever with NASCAR that would indicate that they are changing the status of their support for Rainbow/PUSH." Farrell added that they "were looking forward to working with NASCAR on future diversity projects."[3]

Farrell talked to the media several days after NASCAR insisted the support had ended.

Then-NASCAR President Mike Helton said the donations to Jackson's group were part of an overall plan to increase minority participation in the sport. NASCAR has set up a minority internship program and created secondary education scholarships, and contributed to the Urban Youth Racing School in Philadelphia.

"While we have supported the Rainbow Coalition's work on diversity issues, we do not endorse many of Rev. Jackson's political views or any other political views," Helton said in his April 23, 2003 statement.

In keeping with its clandestine methods of trying to erase stock car's racial stigma, NASCAR also sidled into the local Daytona Beach mayoral contest. In a series of unprecedented meetings held on company grounds in 2003, Bill France Jr. repeatedly urged employees who lived in the city to vote for Yvonne Scarlet-Golden, a black, 77-year-old councilwoman. He called her the best candidate, even though other younger, more qualified people were running for the office. He also repeatedly declined to explain why the company was supporting Golden, a nice person but someone who seemed too old for the position. She eventually died in office after being re-elected to a second two-year term.

Employees were given time off to volunteer for the Golden campaign, and the creative staff produced advertising and brochures. Spending was estimated at $200,000, not including unaccounted staff time, the kind of largess unheard of in any previous local mayoral campaign.

The local newspaper suggested the investment was aimed at securing good terms when the Daytona International Speedway lease came up for renewal. That turned out to be incorrect; the lease remains valid for another 25 years. The real cause was that Golden is black, and NASCAR was smarting from the racist accusations.

In June 2003, Rainbow/PUSH board member Bill Shack called auto racing "the last bastion of white supremacy" in professional sports, and Rainbow Sports director Ferrell blasted NASCAR by labeling it "a good ole' boy's Southern cracker sport" in July.

In response, France could point to Golden and insist the company was not racist.

That won't work nationally. Given the changing demographics in this country, NASCAR will have to build bridges to the minority community long before it becomes the majority or face a slow, inevitable dissipation of its popularity.

"We can do all advertising we can do reaching out to African-American fans," said Humpy Wheeler, president of Lowe's Motor Speedway. "But when we have one that starts winning, that's what's going to break it wide open."

That hasn't happened yet.

NASCAR has suspended two people for using racial slurs since 2009, a driver and a crew chief. In 2004, NASCAR also initiated a diversity program to develop minority and female drivers. It hasn't done much. No person in the program from 2004 to 2009 is currently driving in any top NASCAR series. It was then revamped and has produced Wallace, Xfinity driver Daniel Suarez and Cup driver Kyle Larson, a Japanese-American racer who was 2015 Sprint Cup rookie of the year.

In addition, NASCAR hired Dr. Richard Lapchick, director of the Institute for Diversity and Ethics in Sports, to join the league's diversity council and give each NASCAR employee diversity training. However, NASCAR won't let Lapchick include stock care racing in his institute's annual racial and gender report card, which studies the makeup and hiring practices of major U.S. sports leagues.

Lapchick also has never presented diversity training to individual NASCAR teams, which hires the drivers.

Moreover, fans who attend the races are overwhelmingly white despite an occasional Xfinity race in Mexico and efforts to attract minority drivers. Some 24 percent of fans maybe black, as NASCAR claims, but they don't go to races. According to a 2013 Nielson study, 94 percent of the TV viewers for the Sprint Cup Series races were white — the highest of any major American sport. Only 2 percent were black.

As a result, the sport has a long way to go. After all, Confederate flags still fly in the infields of some tracks across the South.

Money

It costs a lot of money to compete in the top NASCAR series. Competitive changes introduced in 2004 didn't help. The new aerodynamic rules and softer tires actually boosted costs an estimated $1 million.

More recently, NASCAR has tried a new tact. In 2016, created franchises. Instead of the independent contractor model that Bill France incorporated, NASCAR awarded 32 franchises. Two went to defunct Michael Waltrip Racing (MWR), which went out of business in 2015.

With a franchise, a team is guaranteed income and a spot in the field.

Team owners liked the idea. For example, MWR co-owner Rob Kauffman sold his franchises to other teams. "I think we've put teams on a more stable footing," Kauffman said.

At the same time, the deal gave new credibility to the Race Team Alliance, which was formed by several team owners and negotiated the deal with NASCAR officials. In the past, Bill France rejected any such union-like activity, but NASCAR has been forced to change as economic pressure increases.

The franchises come with stipulations: they can only be sold once in five years; they only last nine years; and teams must compete every week. Only teams that entered drivers since 2013 were eligible to be awarded a franchise. If a team didn't get a franchise, it can buy one or attempt to qualify in one of the four available spots each week. The Wood Brothers, one of NASCAR's oldest teams, finds itself in that unenviable position even though the team planned to run all races in 2016.

It's too early to see if the franchise approach will help reduce costs. Still, something had to be done.

Team owner Richard Childress, who fields cars in each of NASCAR's three national touring series and employs hundreds of people, said costs are getting out of hand. "It's just tougher and tougher today to make it, even with a sponsorship," he said. "You just got to do everything you can to get enough revenue to be competitive today." [4]

The problem is widespread. "It may be too soon to call it a crisis, but there is definitely a financial crunch facing NASCAR's teams." [5]

Although estimates vary, top teams reportedly get up to $35 million from sponsors for prime advertising sites on cars — the hood, rear deck and quarter panels. Smaller sponsors will pay $250,000 to $2 million for decals elsewhere on the vehicle.

It sounds like a lot of money, but still doesn't cover all the expenses.

Childress said his company still has to fund about 30 percent of its budget from other sources. "You've got to do it through endorsements, royalties, race winnings, TV money and leasing engines," he said. "And it's tougher and tougher to do that." 6

As a result, fewer teams are available to compete each week. To counter that, in 2016 NASCAR trimmed the field from the traditional 43 cars to 40. Actually, 43 was never a sacrosanct number. In the early, years, the list of competitors depended basically on who showed up. NASCAR settled on a field set at 43 starting in 1998 — supposedly because that was Richard Petty's car number.

NASCAR really had no choice. In 2004, only 46 cars vied for the 43 starting spots in the Daytona 500, even though Mark Martin took home $195,663 for finishing last.

In the final race of 2015, the Ford Econoboost 400, which drew national attention with four drivers competing for the championship, the field was littered with unknown drivers such as Michael Annett, Matt DiBenedetto and Ryan Preece, all needed to fill out the field. None finished higher than 30.

That continued the NASCAR tradition of having "fillers" to complete the mandated 43-car fields. Veteran drivers like Joe Ruttman, Andy Hillenburg, Kirk Shelmerdine and Carl Long simply started and drove enough to collect checks for competing. Ruttman, who turned 60 in 2004, came to one race without a pit crew. He still won close to $400,000, despite never finishing better than 41st in seven races that year.

Regular drivers complained that the fillers were too slow, even though, on occasion, they posted decent results. They could be an obstacle, however. At Darlington Raceway in the 2004 spring race, Tony Stewart ran into the back of Andy Hillenburg, who then spun around and was mashed by Jeff Gordon. Both Gordon and Stewart are members of top teams and would eventually finish in the top 10 in the championship standings.

Hillenburg, who supports his racing habit with funds from

his own company, insisted the accident was his fault, saying he drifted up in front of Stewart and hoped "his team would soon build him a better car."

Gordon countered, "I know it's not Andy Hillenburg's fault, but there are a lot of guys out there who shouldn't be — they're just so far off the pace."

The high costs have affected top drivers and teams, too. Mike Skinner, Todd Bodine and Jimmy Spencer are just a few of the drivers in recent years who lost rides when sponsorship dried up. Dale Earnhardt Inc. (DEI) dropped John Andretti in 2004 when Pennzoil pulled its backing from the No. 1 Chevrolet. Veteran Bill Elliott, once the most popular driver in NASCAR history, decided to reduce his schedule in 2004, but could not enter as many races as he wanted because his team could not locate even a part-time sponsor.

Ward Burton, a former Daytona 500 winner, sat out a year and never came back.

Some teams are relying on split sponsorships between non-competitive companies. Matt Kenseth, the 2003 NASCAR Sprint Cup champion, was sponsored by both Smirnoff Ice and DeWalt Tools. NASCAR has a long-standing policy against allowing hard liquor companies to sponsor race teams, but that changed as the economy soured. In 2004, champion Kurt Busch was sponsored by Irwin Tools and Sharpie Pens.

In 2016, most teams have multiple sponsors, including Ty Dillon (Kleenex/Kroger), Jimmie Johnson (Lowe's/Kobalt Tools), Dale Earnhardt Jr. (Nationwide/Mountain Dew/Axalta Coatings Systems/TaxSlayer.com) and Danica Patrick (Nature's Bakery/Aspen Dental/Tax Act/Mobil1). Kevin Harvick's team pierced together five sponsors as did rookie Brian Scott.

Only Casey Mears (Geico), David Ragan (Dr. Pepper), Trevor Bayne (Advocate) and Paul Menard (Menard's) are listed as having a single sponsor. Mears has since been released.

NASCAR feigns a lack of concern.

"We're in the best shape that we've been in a long time," Bill France Jr. said more than a decade ago. "It doesn't mean that we're perfect." France said it seems like every year one or two good teams lack a sponsor. "But look at the vast majority of the teams," he said. "They are sponsored, and that is coming out of a choppy economy." [7]

Today, that optimism seems misguided.

Cost are not dropping. The sanctioning body will have to find other ways to cut expenditures. Otherwise, fewer companies will be able to fully fund teams, leading to a decline in competition between the top and secondary teams and a return to the days when only a handful of teams could possibly win a race. Competition drives the sport; lack of competition will strangle it.

Changes

NASCAR fans love consistency. NASCAR apparently does not. The sanctioning body shrugged off criticism and ended the heritage-rich Southern 500 by shifting the hallowed race from creaky Darlington Raceway in 2004 to the much newer California Speedway.

Road courses, once a staple of NASCAR, have been reduced to two venues.

The company no longer owns its own radio network, having sold that. It doesn't produce its own race programs. That division was sold off, too. Tradition simply doesn't mean as much to NASCAR as money.

Some of the biggest changes were initiated in the last 15 years with the addition of the playoff system in 2004. The new approach as designed to prevent someone from winning the title without capturing a single checkered flag. It had to be tinkered with. After all, in 2014, Ryan Newman could have won the title without winning a single race. So, for 2015, drivers who won races automatically advanced, and losers were dropped from the playoffs.

Of course, that was not set in concrete. Kyle Busch, who missed time because of a broken leg, was allowed to finish at least 30th in the standings and qualify for the playoffs. He succeeded and eventually won the title. The same opportunity was accorded Tony Stewart in 2016.

NASCAR also introduced the Car of Tomorrow in 2007, which was supposed to be simpler and less expensive, but was boxier, didn't handle well and offered limited manufacturer identity. By 2013, NASCAR brought the next version on board in 2013

The various alterations, done without consultation with the competitors, have left some drivers fuming.

"In a way, NASCAR is kind of like the mafia," Stewart told ESPN radio in spring 2004. "They can do it any way they want to do it. They know we make a better living doing this the way it is than we could anywhere else, and whether we have an opinion or not, it doesn't seem to matter — they're going to run it they want to run it."

Stewart, who announced his retirement for the end of the 2016 season, was realistic about the situation. "Unfortunately, in this day and age, it's about dollars and sense, not what's good for the race fans, what's good for the competitors, not what's good for everybody else involved, just what's good for them."

He was probably even more upset after 2006 when he finished the first 26 races in 11th place, one spot out of the title run. In response, at the end of the year, NASCAR arbitrarily increased the championship field to 12. Now, 16 drivers are included.

That radical alteration led to dissension and competition. Several promoters announced plans for a new national stock car series, but it fizzled. Stewart didn't expect it to last anyway or have any impact on NASCAR.

"From what I've seen of NASCAR," he said, "they're pretty hardheaded and set in their ways. Their approach is, 'It's our way or the highway.' I might be driving down the highway pretty soon." [8]

Stewart is outspoken and has opposed other NASCAR moves, including mandating head-and-shoulder safety devices. That doesn't mean the remaining drivers don't agree with him.

Change is axiomatic in any sport: baseball added designated hitters; basketball drew a three-point line, etc. Still, radical change usually takes time and much debate, except in stock car racing. NASCAR's director, Brian France, wanted something different, so the scoring format was altered. Simple as that.

Hero

As noted in the last chapter, Dale Earnhardt's death removed the man driving NASCAR's surging popularity. Bill Elliott may have continually won the Most Popular Driver award, but fans came to root for and against Earnhardt.

His son assumed the mantle, but who was next in line? That's a troubling question now, highlighted by the falloff in interest when Earnhardt Jr. sat out the last half of the 2016 season with concussion-like symptoms. NASCAR knows fully well the impact when a top driver departs. Now, Jeff Gordon has basically retired, except for filling in for Earnhardt Jr. on occasion. Tony Stewart is retiring.

Who's left?

NASCAR can only hope that one of the young drivers, such as Austin Dillon, whose car carries Earnhardt's old No. 3, steps up. So far, none have. NASCAR's effort to make cars more equal and improve competition has meant that more drivers win. If no one dominates, no one attracts wide support. One possibility, Danika Patrick, drew public attention because of her looks, not for her on-track success. That's not what NASCAR needs for the long run.

Race officials are fully aware what happened when Tiger Woods dropped off the PGA circuit. Viewership of the 2014 Master's without Woods dropped to 1957 levels, when professional golf rarely earned more an a blip of coverage. "Tiger Woods still is professional golf," wrote to freelance sportswriter Jas Notte. "Overall, Golf.com places his value to the sport at around $15 billion. That's 22 percent of the $68.8 billion golf industry and roughly a quarter of the status quo that isn't coming back if millennials and other casual fans tune out golf altogether."[9]

That same thing could happen to NASCAR, whose fans are much older. In fact, only golf has older fans. NASCAR fans remember Dale Earnhardt, Jeff Gordon in his heyday and even Richard Petty. Without someone of that caliber showing up, younger fans won't be drawn to the sport, and the crowds in the stands, already thinning, will get even sparser.

Monopoly situations

Although NASCAR is not the only stock car sanctioning body, it dominates the field and dictates the rules. However, such controlling organizations tend to fall apart over time. Racing on a road with strange twists and curves, NASCAR can't afford to lose control. Its future, and the future of stock car racing, could be at stake.

After all, based on past history, another turn is likely coming up soon.

SOURCES

Chapter 1: 1895

1 http://www.autoswalk.com/durmontwag.html
2 Duryea, Frank, America's First Automobile (1942); Berkebile, Don H., The 1893 Duryea Automobile, Contributions From the Museum of History and Technology vol. 240, Smithsonian Institution (1966).

Chapter 2: 1938

1 http://www.indianapolismotorspeedway.com/ims/companies/history.php
2 http://motorsportsnews.net/rs20040301.html
3 http://insiderracingnews.com/om071802.html
4 http://www.arcaracing.com/Remax/dirthardin02.html
5 Woody, Larry, Auto Racing Digest, May 2001
6 Willis, Ken http://www.news-journalonline.com/speed/special/2003/speedDTAB1930.htm February 12, 2003

Chapter 3: 1950

1 Conley, Kevin, New Yorker, August 18, 25, 2003
2 Oldham, Scott http://popu
3 Christ, Bob http://www.thedailystar.com/sports/2001/09/01/spbob.html
4 Bechtel, Mark http://www.cnnsi.com/magazine/features/si50/states/south_carolina/hearts_ racing/ September 8, 2003
5 Pearce, Al, Daily Press, March 22, 2003
6 Christ, September 2, 2000

7   Ralstin, Dick http://home.flash.net/~dralstin/stories/Darlington-Plymouth.htm

8   Pearce

9   http://popularmechanics.com/automotive/motor_sports/1998/8/nascar_turns_50/print.phtml

Chapter 4: 1969

1   http://extras.journalnow.com/lostempire/tob13a.htm

Chapter 5: 1979

1   http://k92fm.com/common/racing/static/history.html December, 2001

2   ps://books.google.com/books?id=uCyjVKHVpNkC&pg=PA126&lpg=PA126&dq=how+many+

3   Pearce, A1, Daily Press, March 23, 2003

4   Martin, Ace, http://www.maximonline.com/sports/articles/article_328.html September 1998

Chapter 6: 1984

1   Kurth, Joanne, St. Petersburg Times. Oct.2, 2002 www.sptimes.com/2002/10/7/Sports/For_Jeff_Gordon__a_su.shtml - 42k -

2   The Associated Press, Oct. 16, 2004

3   www.bayarea.com/mld/mercurynews/sports/3528683.htm

4   www.thatsracin.com/mld/thatsracin/archives/3315023.htm

5   Puma, Mike, ESPN.Com espn.go.com/classic/biography/s/Gordon_Jeff.html

6   Jenkins Chris USA Today, July 12, 2002 www.usatoday.com/sports/motor/ nascar/2002-07-12-acov-sponsors.htm

7   Ibid

8   Puma

9   www.gordonline.com/busch/bgn92.html

10   Puma

11   Puma

12   Puma

13   Fortune April 12, 1999 v139 i7, p56+

14   Ibid

15   Ibid

16   Ibid

17 Ibid

Chapter 7: 2001

1   Van Dyck, Dave, FOXSports.Com, February 18, 2001
    http://www2.foxsports.com/obits/earnhardt/vandy2.sml
2   Rovell, Darren, ESPN.com http://espn.go.com/classic/
    s/2001/0222/1101909.html
3   Forbeshttp://www.forbes.com/lists/2004/10/25/
    cx_2004deadcelebtears_16.ht3 3 Van Dyke
4   http://www.circletrack.com/eventcoverage/13479/
5   http://www.guardian.co.uk/elsewhere/journalist/
    story/0,7792,440456,00.html
6   Harris, Mike, Associated Press, Feb. 19, 2001
7   Fowler, Scott, The Charlotte Observer, February 27, 2001
8   Korth, Joanne, St. Petersburg Times, March 9, 2002
9   Fryer, Jenna, Associated Press
10 http://nascar.about.com/library/weekly/aa031201a.htm
11 Korth, Joanne, St. Petersburg Times, July 3, 2002

Chapter 8: 2004

1   http://www.playboy.com/features/features/daleearnhardtjr/ Sept.
    2001
2   By Marty Smith, Turner Sports Interactive, February 17, 2004\
3   http://www.cnnsi.com/racing/specials/daytona500/2004/
4   http://www.nascar.com/2004/news/headlines/official/05/26/
    dearnhardtjr_qa/
5   Harris, Mike, CBS News http://www.cbsnews.com/
    stories/2004/02/16/entertainment/main600449.shtml
6   Harris
7   Associated Press, February 16, 2004
8   http://www.nascar.com/2004/news/headlines/official/05/26/
    dearnhardtjr_qa/
9   Korth, Joanne, St. Petersburg Times
    http://www.sptimes.com/2002/10/06/Sports/Earnhardt_Jr_can_t_
    ou.shtml October 6, 2002
10 Korth
11 Korth

Chapter 9: Future

1   http://www.racinglimos.com/motorsports_popularity.phtml?id=26
    August 2004
2   http://www.aaregistry.com/african_american_history/1109/
    Black_race_car_legend_Wendell_O_Scott 2004
3   Jenkins, Chris USA Today
    http://www.usatoday.com/sports/motor/nascar/2003-07-28-jack-
    son-support_x.htm
4   http://www.nascar.com/2004/news/headlines/cup/04/10/nascar_
    costs/ 2004
5   Harris Mike, The Associated Press March 25, 2004
    http://www.nascar.com/2004/news/headlines/cup/03/25/bc.car..
    nascar.sellingca.ap/
6   Harris
7   Jenkins
    http://www.usatoday.com/sports/motor/nascar/2004-02-12-
    france-1acover_x.htm
8   Bonkowski, Jerry ESPN.com
    http://espn.go.com/rpm/wc/2001/1012/1263034.html
9   http://www.marketwatch.com/story/without-tiger-woods-golf-is-
    fading-to-gray-2015-04-17

ABOUT
THE AUTHOR

Bill Lazarus has been a veteran NASCAR historian whose book, *The Sands of Time, Celebrating 100 years of Racing in Daytona*, was first published in 2004. A second edition was published in 2016. A native of Maine, he served as a reporter and editor for several newspapers and magazines, spent five years as editorial manager for ISC Publications, producing programs for races, and has taught writing classes at Embry-Riddle Aeronautical University, Daytona Beach (Fla.) Community College and in high school.

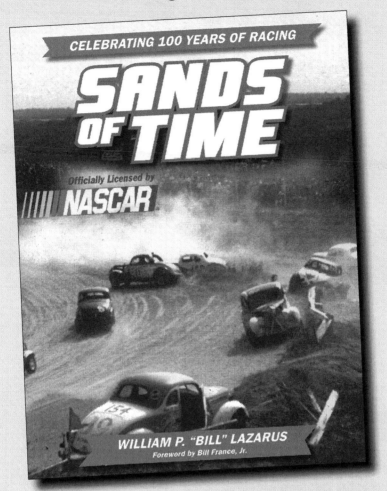

Other books by William P. Lazarus ...

Adventures in Bonding

Fiction / Adventure / Humor

Bond? James Bond? He couldn't be James Bond, and probably wasn't. Unfortunately for Police Sgt. Mc-Connell, the mystery man believes he is the legendary secret agent, and he can't be dismissed with a shaken-not-stirred vodka martini and a pat on the head. He has information regarding a murder, and he won't reveal anything unless she plays along. But things get serious when "Bond" starts taking chances with their lives—and the culprits are playing for keeps!

Ice Flow

Fiction / Drama

Revere River seemed like a good idea. Then, everything went down-hill—like the population, which grew weary of the unrelenting snow; the avalanche that killed another chunk of the population; the economy, which relied on outlaws seeking solitude, and the annual gathering of bounty hunters to clear them out. Now a slick shyster keeps the town in his hip pocket—and the town may crack like ice.

www.boldventurepress.com

Made in the USA
Columbia, SC
29 January 2024

30815240R00091